SUPERNATURAL
ON STAGE

Also by Richard Huggett

SUPERNATURAL ON STAGE

GHOSTS AND SUPERSTITIONS OF THE THEATRE

RICHARD HUGGETT

TAPLINGER PUBLISHING COMPANY | NEW YORK

First Edition

Published in the United States in 1975 by
TAPLINGER PUBLISHING CO., INC.
New York, New York

Published simultaneously in the Dominion of Canada by
Burns & MacEachern, Ltd, Toronto

Library of Congress Catalog Card Number: 73-16966

ISBN 0-8008-7495-1

Designed by Mollie M. Torras

*I dedicate this book to the spirit of goodness
as enshrined in the figure of the White Goddess,
the Virgin Mary . . . may she protect it against
the Devil and all his works.*

Acknowledgments

A special word of thanks to the following for their kindness and generosity in giving so much of their time and taking so much trouble for me while I was writing *Supernatural on Stage:* Dr. Carl Meyer, Lincoln Center Drama Collection, New York; Louis Rachow, Walter Hampden Library, Players Club, New York; George Nash and Tony Lathom of the Enthoven Collection, London.

So many other people have helped in one way or another and have contributed such valuable services, that to acknowledge properly what they have done would take another book. I hope they will forgive me if I can only list their names at the back of this book.

RICHARD HUGGETT

Contents

Illustrations

SUPERNATURAL ON STAGE

ONE

Superstitions in the Theatre

Of all professional bodies, actors are the most superstitious, a fact which is freely, indeed cheerfully, admitted. It is interesting to speculate why this should be so, and the answer must surely lie in the character of the actor, and the rather peculiar nature of our work. Actors have a strong imagination and a sense of fantasy: this is essential, otherwise we could not be actors. We tend to be highly strung, nervous, optimistic, apprehensive, sensitive, and credulous. Underneath whatever facade of lively smiling confidence we choose to show to the world, there is often a bottomless pit of hopes, fears, insecurity, and tensions. We live on whatever talents and wits a mainly benevolent Deity has seen fit to give us, and if our work does sometimes offer artistic satisfaction, it never guarantees security, a serious handicap to those encumbered with wives, children, and domestic responsibilities. Poverty, neglect, and frustration alternate in an actor's life with affluence, fame, and fulfillment. If actors live to please, then they must please to live, and we must please not only the public and the critics, but also—and this is sometimes more important—our employers, past, present, and future.

If an actor is different from other people, then it is because his work is like nobody else's. Nobody who has never acted can have the least idea what it means to step onto a stage in front of an audience. Our lives consist of a series of painful and nerve-racking climaxes whether it is the first take in a film, the recording of a radio documentary, a television play going out live or—and this is the worst of all by far—the big First Night in a West End or Broadway threatre. An actor is under continual strain: he lives on his nerves: and in contradiction of the popular, glamorous image, his life is a very difficult one, irrespective of whether he is humble novice, esteemed supporting actor, popular leading man, or international superstar. Everybody wants good luck and dreads bad luck, but in few people is the desire so urgent or the fear so passionate as in an actor facing his nightly ordeal. Is it any wonder that we tend to be superstitious?

It is a gross and insulting oversimplification to describe actors as just so many children playing at make-believe, but there is, surely, a childlike simplicity and emotional naïveté—irrespective of education, intelligence, and background—which transforms the whole of our glittering world into a highly sophisticated and enchanting game of "Let's Pretend." The theatre is an enclosed, isolated world with its own rules and laws, its own traditions and disciplines; and however accurately it may appear to mirror real life it is, in fact, obstinately and justly cut off from it. The sailor, soldier, airman, coal miner, steeplejack, fisherman, all these people lead dangerous lives and are naturally superstitious, but it is not our bodies which we actors endanger, but our hearts and souls; it is not bullets nor storms nor bombs nor cave-ins we fear, but the most deadly and unpredictable and relentless of all natural forces—public opinion and fashion. It is precisely in this sort of artistic and emotional hothouse that superstitions take root and flourish.

Most actors have a talisman, a lucky mascot, which they keep in their dressing rooms and will take religiously from theatre to theatre, from TV to film studio. A random survey of the mascots belonging to a number of stars and lesser luminaries has produced some intriguing items. Wilfrid Hyde White has a collection of chain ornaments; there is a pigeon with a broken beak, a recumbent cow, a pig, an American silver dollar, and, most highly prized of all, a beautiful framed colored photograph of his Rolls-Royce. Every evening, before each entrance, and it doesn't matter how many there are, he will kiss each of these mascots, "all presents from present friends and past mistresses," he smilingly states. Each is gently touched in loving valediction before he leaves the theatre at night. Alec Macowan clings to a navy-blue blazer which he first wore fifteen years ago in *The Elder Statesman*. "You look like a secondhand car salesman" was Henry Sherek's (the producer) acid comment when he appeared with it at the dress rehearsal. He also has a pair of gold cuff links, a present from the grateful American producer of *Hadrian VIII* which he hoped would turn out to be lucky, but it turned out that they were not lucky, so he has since abandoned them. Amanda Reiss also possesses a sartorial mascot, a blue and black checked dressing gown. This was a present from her mother in 1961 when she made her West End debut in *The Irregular Verb to Love*. She wears it to make up in and to receive her visitors after the performance. It is now showing its age and looking rather tatty, but she will never part with it. Cardew Robinson treasures a magnificent color portrait of Bransby Williams in the character of Chief Sitting Bull, donated by a group of friends who know of his fanatical interest in American Indians. Thora Hird always wears under her stage costume three large nappy pins which she once pinned to her daughter, Janette Scott, and her two granddaughters. Jill Bennett's dressing table is covered with lucky mascots—a silver ashtray with a 1936 penny welded to the base, donated and signed by the late Sir Godfrey Tearle; a green china boot given by Royal Ballet dancer, Donald Macleary; a little Oriental knife

Tallulah Bankhead was a walking encyclopedia of superstitions. "You name it, honey, I believe in it," she used to say. Champagne was lucky and must be consumed in quantity before and during a performance. Visitors to her dressing room must always enter with the right foot first; the left foot was unlucky and any offender must be sent out and told to reenter correctly. But her favorite mascot was a hare's foot given to her by her father in 1936. She took it everywhere and it can be seen in the final photo of Brendan Gill's book on her. After her death it was put into the coffin and buried with her. Walter McGinn likes to have a poem written especially for him. The length, subject, and authorship isn't important as long as it's delivered to the theatre for the opening night. Over the years he has accumulated an interesting collection. Ann Rogers once consulted the astrologer, Maurice Woodruff, before accepting an offer to play in *No No Nanette* in Chicago, because she also wanted to play it in London later in the year and did not know if she would be available. Woodruff predicted that the Chicago run would be off in time for her to take up the London offer, and so it was. After that she invariably consulted Woodruff before making any serious decision in her career. His death left a painful gap in the lives of many stars.

Gerry Jedd once found a four-leaf clover in Central Park on her way to an audition for the London production of *Two for the Seesaw*. It was a good audition and she was invited to give another. On her way to the second she found a six-leaf clover in the park. The second audition was very successful and two months later she found herself costarring with Peter Finch at the Haymarket Theatre. She thus enjoyed every unknown's dream of success and overnight stardom. Throughout the six-month run in London she kept the two clovers, but she died at a tragically early age before she could repeat her success.

The three Barrymores, John, Ethel, and Lionel, were very generous to one another but seldom to outsiders. Charity most definitely began at home and stayed there. They invariably gave red apples to one another on their opening nights which must on no account be eaten. This was a very old, very personal family superstition and inherited from their theatrical parents, the famous Drews. It was John who took this one inevitable stage further; on opening nights he drank a jug of apple cider, before and during the performance. A caretaker who once drank it by mistake was instantly dismissed.

Some of the old American vaudeville performers on the touring circuit had some very strange personal superstitions. Jack Pearl used to touch his ear for good luck, but if anybody else did it, he would have to touch the other person's ear before he could go onto the stage. One practical joker who knew this did touch Jack's ear on a very important Broadway opening and then ran away. Jack went berserk and followed him out of the theatre and all round the block before he finally managed to catch up with him.

Jimmy Durante was once asked if he was superstitious. "If I get a cold in da mose and I hear a raven croaking at da same time, then dat means trouble," was his characteristic reply; but there was one he didn't talk about. He was very superstitious about hats which must not on any account be placed on a bed. The only antidote to the bad luck is to take the hat off the bed and hang it up, and it must not be touched until the owner is wearing another. One day, when on tour, his friends in the company played a wicked joke. They bought twenty-five hats and placed them all on the bed in his hotel room and then retired to the bathroom to observe his reaction. This, when he arrived on the scene, caused boundless hilarity and thus added one more item to the Durante legend.

If bad luck can attach itself to beds and items of clothing, then gloves are no exception. The University of Pennsylvania Library claims that it possesses Shakespeare's own gloves (authority unstated!) and tells all visitors that anybody who wears them will die within the year. Maurice Evans was shown them whilst on a wartime tour and was asked if he would like to try them on for size. He refused because, he said, if the gloves were not genuine,

Tallulah Bankhead was a walking encyclopedia of superstitions.

then it was a waste of time, and if they were, then it was sacrilege. He firmly stated that he was not superstitious, but the fact that he was currently appearing in and as *Macbeth* may possibly have influenced his decision. When all's said and done, there is really no point in tempting providence.

Sometimes there are ad hoc mascots for special occasions. Denis Shaw remembers that he was once rehearsing a melodrama called *Barren Soil*, playing an Irish boy called Mad Matt. During the rehearsals he was very bad, couldn't get the feel of the part or come to grips with it, and worked himself up to a state of trembling apprehension about the first performance. A sympathetic old actor, seeing his distress, lent a special pair of cuff links in the shape of a shamrock. The psychological effect was immediate. "I cheered up right away," said Shaw, "and I was *superb!*" June Grey, a variety artiste, once picked up a rusty nail in the wings while waiting to make her first appearance in a provincial pantomime. The evening was a great success and ever since she has always picked up rusty nails. She keeps them in a trunk which travels everywhere with her and is now imbued with good luck. Jack Pearl always picked up pins, good-luck pins, ordinary pins, safety pins, nappy pins, and if the point is toward him as he stoops to pick it up, then this is particularly good luck.

Many actors like to carry their lucky mascots onto the stage whenever possible. Sometimes it is a coin or a ring or a tiny framed photo of their loved one or a hare's foot or a strip of yellow ribbon or a playing card—the queen of spades, in spite of Pushkin, carries good luck associations for many people—or a fragment of costume from a previously lucky play or a tiny teddy bear (very popular as lucky mascots). There is just one rather unfortunate thing about lucky mascots and that is that they can backfire in the most unpleasant and unpredictable way as with a certain young actor whom I shall call Walter Plinge. Walter's lucky mascot was a 1930s dinky car, a souvenir of a happy boyhood. It measured four inches by two and fitted comfortably into his pocket. Throughout his professional career he wore it in the pocket of whatever costume he wore, and if there was none, then the wardrobe mistress would have to improvise one. One day he found himself playing Ariel in a touring production of *The Tempest*, and the costume, as he found to his alarm on the day of the dress rehearsal, was that irreducible, pre-*Oh! Calcutta!* minimum, the skintight jockstrap. The director knew about his dinky car. "Well, dear boy," he inquired sardonically, "just where are you going to put it tonight?" Walter smiled sheepishly. "There's only one place," he said firmly, and he put it there. The result provoked from its first-night audience not only crude laughter but also some rather bawdy anatomical speculation. But there was worse to come. The director had at one time been a choreographer and was very balletically-minded. He had devised some spectacular *grands jetés, arabesques,* and *cabrioles* for Walter who, while executing one of these, stumbled against a rock and fell flat on his face, thus doing himself what is tactfully described as a Mischief. Doubled up, groaning, and clutching himself in agony, Walter was carried offstage by Prospero and Caliban and spent the rest of the evening in the local hospital.

Religious medals are popular, particularly those of St. Genesius, the patron saint of actors. St. Christopher inspires considerable devotion among actors, and there are many who would no more walk on stage than they would embark on a jet liner without their St. Christopher medal. These must be carried on the person and must be blessed. St. Christopher's absence on a critical first night can fill the unhappy performer with real agonizing fear. Kathie Warren, who used to do a William Tell act on ice in which her partner, Scott, would leap over her and slice the apple in two with his razor-blade-sharp ice skates, invariably carried a St. Christopher medal.

Broadway actors talking about their own special superstitions will always come to the famous Gypsy Robe. Gypsy refers to the singing and dancing chorus of the big musicals; the gypsies are the toughest, most hard-working, most fiercely dedicated bunch of professionals on Broadway, and the American theatre's debt to them is incalculable. The Gypsy Robe is a dressing gown covered with souvenirs of previous musicals, and is passed from one company to another. On the first night of a new musical, the current owner brings it to the theatre and presents it to a gypsy in the new show. It can be given to anybody, man or woman. The lucky recipient will put on the robe and parade round the stage so that everybody can see it. Sometimes the company will assemble on the stage to witness the ritual, sometimes the Gypsy will visit all the dressing rooms so that everybody can see it and touch it for luck. Once this has been completed to everybody's satisfaction, the show can go on in an atmosphere of confidence. The Gypsy keeps the robe in his dressing room until the next Broadway musical opens. He then pins or sews some small souvenir of his own show. It might be a program, a photo of the star, or a piece of costume or a small prop, appropriately marked with the name of the show and the date. He will then take it round to the new theatre and pass it on to the Gypsy of his choice. To receive the Gypsy Robe is a colossal honor, though nobody knows who will get it until it arrives.

I was given a privileged glimpse of this unusual ritual on the first night of *Molly* at the Alvin Theatre in October 1973. This was arranged by the assistant director, Jay Fox, and his wife, Bonnie Walker. An attractive young dancer from *Raisin*, Renée Rose, was the previous owner, and she brought it round to the stage door of the Alvin. Surrounded by the electricians, stagehands, the press, and the producer's party of friends, she solemnly presented it to a young dancer, Don Bonnell. Speechless with delight, he wore it, posed for photographs, and then toured the dressing rooms where he was kissed, hugged, touched, and generally made much of by a laughing, crying, highly emotional company. The robe was a very handsome garment and very heavy. On it were attached a sword and coffin (*Cry for Us All*), a balloon (*Gantry*), gold tapes (*No No Nanette*), a tambourine (*Coco*), gold hand prints (*Applause*), a coat of arms with money (*The

Rothschilds), Danny Kaye's photo (*Two by Two*), and a fragment of birthday cake (*Company*).

Molly was based on a popular TV series, "The Goldbergs," and starred the popular and immensely vital Kay Ballard. On the opening night, it was performed with enormous gusto, received with hysterical delight, was later described by the *New York Post* as a warmed-up corpse, and was withdrawn within a month. All of which goes to show that even the angels of luck will take the occasional night off.

The history of the Robe is interesting, and unlike most superstitions its origin can be pinpointed to a place and a date. It started in October 1950 with a chorus singer, Florence Baum, who was appearing in *Gentlemen Prefer Blondes*. She had in her dressing room a white satin gown trimmed with maribou. One of the dancers, Bill Bradley, admired it, and as a rather camp little joke asked permission to wear it backstage to cheer up the other gypsies. The show was a huge success and a week later he sent it round to his friend, Arthur Parrington, who was due to open in *Call Me Madam*. Attached to it was a note saying that this was the famous Gypsy Robe and that to wear it backstage and thus show it to everybody would bring good luck to the show. Arthur Parrington obediently followed the instructions and was delighted that *Call Me Madam* was a huge success also. From then it went to Forrest Bonshire in *Guys and Dolls*, and so the new superstition was kicked off to a flying start. During the years that followed, the original Robe became so encrusted with souvenirs that it began to fall to pieces, and though the wardrobe mistress of *Can Can* in 1953 did her best to sew and darn it together, it finally disintegrated in 1954 and was presented to the Drama Collection in the Lincoln Center where it is occasionally put on show. In twenty-four years there have been no less than five Gypsy Robes; some fall to pieces, some have been lost, one has been stolen.

Claire Bloom never walks on pavement cracks, a childhood superstition which has mysteriously survived into adult life. She touches wood in moments of crisis, as many of us do and—rather curiously—if she accidentally walks under a ladder then she goes straight to bed. Don Fellows was once hampered by a bad stutter. He usually managed to conquer it, but there were good days and bad days. To prepare for a performance, he would perform a little private ritual. He would touch every lamppost on his way to the theatre; if he missed one by chance, then it would be a bad night, but if he managed to touch them all, it would be good! Frankie Vaughan cherishes a silver-topped cane for luck and Ted Lewis once canceled a $5000 engagement because his lucky top hat was lost en route to Chicago. Ed Wynn always wore the same pair of shoes in his act and managed to make one unusually well-made pair last for twenty years.

According to *The New York Times*, good luck could be bought like any other commodity. An advertisement for a Chinese lucky ring selling at a modest price of $1.50 ("Buy NOW to avoid Disappointment!!") found one curious customer in Fanny Brice. Within a week of buying and wearing it, she won $2000 in a lottery. The news spread like wildfire round Broadway, and among those who queued up at the counter at Macy's were W. C. Fields, Francine Larrimore, Robert Mantell, and Raymond Hitchcock. History has not recorded the extent of the luck they were thus able to purchase.

Certain actors and actresses are regarded by their colleagues and employers as lucky mascots: Mrs. Patrick Campbell, Gladys Cooper, and Vivien Leigh all carried with them an aura of imperishable luck and success far in excess of mere stardom, partly owing to their extraordinary beauty and partly their unique talents. All had the ability to drag unlikely and unpromising plays out of the rut and transform them into popular successes. Richard Goolden and Robertson Hare are both regarded as lucky, and producers over the decades have queued up to employ them. Also in this category is the mysterious figure of Walter Plinge, whose identity requires a word of explanation for the public. "Who is Walter Plinge?" is a popular quiz question which recurs with some frequency in the press. In England, if an actor is playing two parts in the same play, the second heavily disguised, he will use a fictitious name in the program to conceal his identity. By a long tradition the name used is Walter Plinge. His appearance on any program was once regarded by his colleagues as a sign of good luck. Actors used to love displaying their versatility at a time when this was encouraged (not so much now, alas), and audiences loved watching it. Mr. Plinge's presence in a play was an indication that the evening was going to be full of old-fashioned theatrical delights. From time to time, the more esoteric magazines will start a correspondence in which Walter Plinge's origins are the subject of learned speculation. Nobody has ever been able to state with certainty when he made his first appearance in the West End, but he is believed to have started his career sometime in the 1870s. Though he never became a star, he acted with the greatest companies, and his career in the profession can be truthfully described as distinguished. At the turn of the century he was very busy and even contrived the major miracle of appearing in three plays simultaneously (did a taxi wait at the stage door to take him from one theatre to the next, one wonders?). During the twenties and thirties he virtually left the West End and acted mainly in the provinces, and after the war his retirement was complete. It is believed that his farewell appearance was in a musical called *Chrysanthemum* at the Apollo in which he played a Dickensian old washerwoman. Few playgoers will forget that supreme *coup de théâtre* when he lifted off his gray wig to reveal the smiling features of Richard Curnock, a popular comedy actor of the postwar years. According to Wilfrid Granville, author of the definitive *Theatrical Dictionary*, the original Walter Plinge was a theatre-crazy landlord who managed a pub opposite the Theatre Royal, Drury Lane, and who extended unlimited credit to the company. Not unnaturally he was greatly liked by them, and one historic Sunday evening they permitted him to satisfy a lifelong ambition by appearing on the stage in a benefit performance given in his honor and under his own name.

In America his equivalent is George Spelvin. As with Walter Plinge his ancestry is obscure, but he is thought to have originally been a member of the Lambs Club. His career didn't last as long as that of his English counterpart, a fact which can only be due to overwork. At one time (1900–1903) he played no less than 210 parts in three years, a fact which, if Equity had existed at that time, would certainly have aroused its sympathetic concern. The Spelvin family, unlike the Plinge family, includes a sister, Georgina Spelvin. She has recently appeared in a very controversial sex film (1973), which is rumored to be the subject of legal action.

Between the wars, the Music Box Theatre in New York boasted a lucky backstage worker. Sam Roseman, master property man, was the object of this belief, and to guarantee success every leading lady had to be photographed sitting on his lap. Margaret Sullavan in *Dinner at Eight* in 1933 started it just as a joke, and it worked. Helen Broderick in *Thousands Cheer*, Tallulah Bankhead in *Rain*, Clare Boothe in *Of Mice and Men*, Martha Scott in *The Male Animal* are only a few of the lucky leading ladies. Nobody knows who started this idea, but it is believed to have been Sam Roseman. In *Ceiling Zero*, there was no leading lady, so Osgood Perkins, the leading man, sat on his lap, but strangely enough this didn't work, and the play was not a success.

So much for the lucky people. Contrariwise, there are unlucky actors who, although dedicated and talented, contrive to bring misfortune to a play and unhappiness to a company. Peter Bull relates how he once accepted a West End engagement and inquired after his colleagues. A list of names was rattled off. "That's not a cast list," he exclaimed in horror, "that's a suicide pact." Kate Claxton, a popular American musical comedy star of the 1890s was thought to be highly unlucky. Her career was dogged by an amazing number of burned-down theatres, train accidents, and other disasters. In spite of this, she was always in work, for she had a superb singing voice, a rare beauty, and, if that wasn't enough, a fair measure of acting ability.

Then there are those first-night rituals that give strength and reassurance and calm the nerves and that are faithfully performed on first nights in the theatre and the taping of TV plays. Not every actor has a ritual, but most of us do, and some of these are exceedingly bizarre. The public misunderstands, for the public doesn't realize what an actor goes through on these distressing occasions. Some of us take it much worse than others. Some actors feel sick, quite literally sick, like Bob Hoskins who has been sick on first nights so many times that he gets worried if he isn't sick, and then somehow has to contrive to make himself sick before he can act. Alec Guinness develops a crippling pain in his knees and back. George Arliss would walk round the theatre several times before he dared enter, not only on first nights, but every night. José Ferrer, by a monumental effort of mind, convinced himself that everybody in the audience was a personal friend. Al Jolson did likewise, which was a little easier in his case as many of them were, and those who weren't, felt that they were. It was a thousand pities that he could never nerve himself to cross the Atlantic and perform in England. Money beyond the dreams of Solomon was laid at his feet for a brief London season, and, after his films were released, his fan mail from England could have left him in no doubt as to the warmth of his reception there, but he regarded foreign appearances as very bad luck, and the thought of appearing in front of a strange audience filled him with superstitious terror. "If there's just one guy who ain't enjoying the show," he once said in explanation, "I'll know it and that'll kill me."

Sir Henry Irving, on first nights, would always walk to the theatre instead of taking a cab as was his custom. From his rooms in Grafton Street to the Lyceum Theatre was a thirty-minute walk, but the exercise calmed his nerves, and the open, unashamed adoration of all he met on this royal progress—paper sellers, flower girls, shopkeepers, ordinary pedestrians—went far to banish the nightmare of insecurity and inadequacy which haunted him throughout his life. He was very popular with the substrata of London life: he tipped them generously, chatted unselfconsciously to them, and generally felt far more at home in their company than with the grander people who filled his theatre. They in turn would cheer and salute him as he walked past, smooth his path, and, in many small ways, look after him. Passing through Covent Garden he would invariably buy a small posy of violets from one of the flower girls there and place it on his dressing table. The sad thing about this routine is that it didn't really help him. Irving was always at his worst on first nights, and one of the reasons was the presence of his wife in the stage box. Although they had parted in 1871 on rather less than amicable terms, and although they never again spoke to each other, Irving continued to discharge what he felt to be his marital duty (or was it a secret masochism rising from God only knows what sense of guilt?) by giving her seats for all his premieres. She would sit there gazing at him with cold, implacable hatred, willing him to fail, and although he was very shortsighted, he never failed to see her.

There are other interesting first-night rituals. Derek Fowldes has a carefully worked-out routine which is not untypical of many actors. He always comes to the theatre a full hour before the performance, reads the evening paper with his feet up, and then has a shower when the half hour is called. He then prepares a drink of honey, lemon, and warm water and luxuriously sips this while making up and dressing. When the five minutes is called, he performs a complicated series of vocal exercises and then takes a tablet of vitamin C. He does all this in the same sequence religiously every night, and although it could be described by cynics as a simple commonsensical way of relaxing, it has, over the years, acquired a definite aura of good luck, and he admits that he would be seriously alarmed if circumstances compelled him to omit any part of it.

Peter Barkworth has a ritual by which he always travels to the theatre by the same route. (Sir John Gielgud, perversely, never does; that's his ritual.) It started when Barkworth was playing at the Savoy in 1955 in *A Woman of No Importance*. He would always travel from St. John's Wood to Trafalgar Square by a 159 bus and then walk down the Strand. But instead of taking the obvious shortcut down by, or through, the Coal Hole Pub, he would go farther along and turn into Savoy Place before going through the stage door. On one memorable occasion he met some of the company on the Embankment whither he had gone to see a film during the afternoon. They were returning to the theatre, and rather than embarrass them, he walked with them to the stage door and then excused himself and dashed up to the Strand and returned to the stage door by his usual route. On the one occasion when he did come by a different route, he gave a bad performance and he has no desire to run the risk of repeating it. He always tries to avoid going past the front of the theatre and, if this is not possible, he takes very good care not to look at the pictures of himself outside. During rehearsals he will never on any account watch the scenes he is not in, nor will he watch other people's scenes on the monitor set when acting in a TV play.

Sir Laurence Olivier states firmly that he is not in any genuine sense of the word superstitious, but he does admit that when driving to the theatre he will look hard at any water of the Thames whenever he drives over it (the water of a river is the bringer of life and thus represents good luck), and if he is passing under a bridge on which a train is passing over, he will not alter speed. Jim Dale is superstitious about clean fingernails and will hold up the curtain if he has not cleaned them. Leslie Phillips jumps up and down in his dressing room and burps, a simple routine which is also used by boxers. Jack Lemmon always whispers the words "magic time" just before the cameras begin to turn, a hangover from his early days in TV. Magic is, after all, what every actor wants to produce and all audiences want to experience. Jenny Laird hypnotizes herself into thinking that it's not her in the part but somebody else, and that she is standing in the wings watching this alter ego; once she has done this, the first night has no further terrors for her. Tilly Losch, Austrian musical star of the twenties and thirties, would never open on October

23, or even go out of her home on that day if she was working. Apparently two near-fatal accidents occurred on October 23 of two consecutive years. The first was a car accident and the second was a fire in her hotel. She escaped from both, but only just, and that particular day clearly has the jinx on it. John Bryans has a very peculiar ritual before he tapes a TV play, which most actors agree is ten times more nerve-racking than a theatrical first night: he goes to the lavatory, sits on the seat, and silently recites the names of actors he admires . . . Wilfrid Walter, Conrad Veidt, Wilfrid Lawson, Donald Wolfit, Henry Ainley. Ken Waller always eats a sweet called Cherry-Ripe, originally supplied by his mother in his early days. He believes that they are good for the voice and, like aspirin, cure headaches and calm the nerves.

Some young actors tend to scoff at superstitions but not Michael Ridgeway who spent three years as the youngest son of the Barrett family in the musical, *Robert and Elizabeth*. He admits to being riddled with irrelevant and illogical superstitions. He is always first out of the dressing room and he likes when possible to dress on the empty stage. He considers it very good luck to iron his trousers on the stage. If he touches something with his left hand while he is dressing, then he must immediately touch the same thing with his right hand: this balances things up, and a good balance between extremes is traditionally good augury. When the call "Beginners, please" is announced three minutes before the opening of the play, he embarks on a curious little ritual. He puts the tips of his fingers together which will store the energy in the tips, holds his cupped hands together, and then follows the line of his fingers upward. He then gazes fixedly at whatever object lies immediately ahead, which might be a picture or a light fitting or a curtain rail. He then looks hard at it and swallows. This gives him that feeling of assurance and confidence without which nobody can act. Alec Macowan has one curious little ritual which is performed not only on first nights but on other occasions of stress. If he is on his way to an interview or audition and he has to cross the road at a pedestrian crossing, he will do so only when the light is green; if he reaches the other side before it changes to red then it will be a lucky day.

Gerry Small, the Jamaican actor, thinks that dressing rooms are unlucky and will avoid them; instead he will prowl round the empty wings where he can be alone. Richard Dennis, following the example of his father, a variety star of the twenties, walks around the empty theatre to get the feel of it. Many actors do this and there is a sound, practical reason for it. Only by this reconnaisance can you discover the size and test the acoustics. Cardew Robinson has a curious superstition about forgotten errands; if he has to return to his dressing room to get something he has forgotten, he will always count ten before going in, though he cannot give a logical explanation for it.

Marlene Dietrich is superstitious about the stars, as are many theatre people. She lives under the sign of Capricorn which she says is not a good zodiac sign but it helps her to organize things—she cannot endure an untidy dressing room, which is bad luck to her, or an untidy stage, which is why her dressing rooms and theatres are always religiously clean. Joe Melia goes one stage further in this; his dressing room is not merely tidy, he likes to keep it in a state of monastic simplicity—functional and unlived in. Not for him the cozy domestic touches whereby most actors like to transform their dressing room into a second home. This bleakness helps him to concentrate and give a good performance. John Graham regards it as very bad luck to consult his script before the performance and banishes it from his dressing room, whereas most actors would die a thousand deaths if it wasn't on their dressing table and wide open for endless consultations. Likewise, having a script on the stage for discreet consultation in a moment of crisis is regarded as very bad luck for some old actors, but actors faced with the nightmare ordeal of a one-man show will usually find a way of getting something on the stage to help them out in an emergency. When I started doing *The First Night of Pygmalion*, in which I was on the stage continuously for

two and a quarter hours, I always had two scripts lying around
the stage disguised as props, and would never think of embarking
on the performance without them. For this reason, I am convinced, the moment of crisis never occurred. Beerbohm Tree
took this one stage further: his first-night memory was so treacherous that he had all the difficult parts written out on separate
pieces of paper and pinned in likely places all round the stage so
that wherever he found himself in trouble, help was near at hand.
Carol Channing stays up all night before an opening, going over
every word. Sir Laurence Olivier did this on the night before his
first *Richard III* at the New Theatre in 1944, a very nerve-racking
and traumatic night, as he was later to remember. *Richard* was the
third play to be launched in the historic Old Vic season. The
other two were *Peer Gynt* and *Arms and the Man*, and they had
been hugely successful. During the dress rehearsals of *Richard*,
Olivier had suffered some alarming lapses of memory which, for
one who enjoys almost photographic recall of the text, was a very
sinister omen. He was filled with a superstitious fear that the play
would be the ugly duckling of the repertoire and that he would
experience a really crucifying failure. The night before the opening he and Vivien Leigh and Garson Kanin went over the whole
part again and again in a suite at Claridges. The rest is history.

The Lunts had two superstitions as I remember well from the
six months I spent with them during the London production of
The Visit in 1960. They would never cross anybody on a staircase,
and I remember a couple of occasions when they insisted, politely
but firmly, on standing on the top stair until I had climbed up and
passed them to the point of safety. My bewilderment clearly
showed and Lynn Fontanne gently explained to me. "It's terribly
bad luck to cross whilst inside in a theatre," she said. "Ellen
Terry told me this and I've never forgotten it." It was strange to
be reminded so directly that she had been a friend of Ellen
Terry's fifty years earlier (and mentioned in that lady's diary),
and it was remarks like this which triggered curious speculation

The Lunts in the Theatre Guild Production of Chekhov's The Sea Gull

among the company as to her age. The theatrical reference books were discreetly silent on the subject, and Lynn Fontanne will doubtless take the secret to her grave. Their other superstition was a very strong belief that it was good luck to come to the theatre at least three hours in advance and sometimes more. For a 7:30 performance they were confortably installed in their two dressing rooms by three in the afternoon. They would have a light lunch, Alfred would read the papers and do the crossword puzzle, and she would get into the rather complicated wig and costume in which she made her first entrance. For two hours they would enjoy a monastic silence and seclusion—and there is nothing more tomblike than an empty theatre. This was their way of soaking up the atmosphere of the play and relaxing.

Contrariwise, Charles Hawtrey, the darling of the Edwardian comedy theatre, believed it to be very bad luck to come early to the theatre, as this gave him plenty of time to get curtain nerves, and, since he was already a very highly strung man, this would effectively stop him from acting well. He liked to appear in the theatre not the usual thirty-five minutes before curtain of theatre tradition and law, but just before his entrance. The stage-door keepers of the different theatres in which he appeared would well remember his nightly arrival. He would rush out of the taxi, through the stage door, down the corridors, and onto the stage, arriving just in time for his first line. This was, of course, a distinctly worrying situation for the stage manager who never knew if Hawtrey would appear or not until he did, so the understudy was kept in a state of permanent readiness. This lateness was against all the accepted rules of the theatre, but since Hawtrey was an actor-manager and his own employer, he was entitled to make and break them to his own satisfaction.

Sir Henry Irving regarded himself as master of his own fate and entirely independent of augury, but a Cornish ancestry and upbringing cannot be lightly cast off. Although his grandson and biographer was unable to find much evidence of a superstitious nature, it seems that he was deeply superstitious about peacocks, and further more he did attach good luck to a little fox terrier called Fussy who was his inseparable companion. Irving lavished on him all the pent-up, frustrated affection which a lonely and loveless man is likely to extend to an animal, and Fussy's death in 1897 was one of the greatest emotional blows he suffered. After that his fortunes declined rapidly; a South London warehouse was burned down and with it the accumulated scenery and costumes and furniture for twenty-five productions, the mainstay of his repertory. A series of unsuccessful productions brought him almost to the point of bankruptcy, and he was finally forced to sell out to a syndicate and was thus no longer master of his own theatre.

Mrs. Patrick Campbell was superstitious about a loathsome little Pekingese called Moonbeam. Her refusal ever to be separated from him even for a moment resulted in her rejecting a number of very lucrative film offers (Mrs. Higgins in *Pygmalion*, Lady Britomart in *Major Barbara*) at a time in her final years when she was suffering great financial hardship. In view of the quality of these two films, both directed by Anthony Asquity, the loss to posterity is beyond calculation.

Barbra Streisand has been reticent on the subject, but she did admit with characteristic humor that she considered it bad luck to step in front of an express train going at eighty miles per hour. Noel Coward once informed the press that the only superstitions he had ever had was that it was bad luck to sleep thirteen in a bed. The laughter which followed encouraged him to repeat the joke in his next play, which was the very successful *Nude with Violin*. Robert Morley has shown a distinct impatience with the existing superstitions and has brought his splendidly creative imagination to bear on the subject. He now invents his own and has firmly announced to the world that it is very bad luck while traveling to the theatre to listen to "The Archers" in the car. It is difficult to avoid the conclusion that other people have brought similar powers of invention when answering my appeal for information. What is one to make of "bad luck to eat peanuts in the dressing room . . .

Mrs. Patrick Campbell as Eliza Doolittle in Pygmalion

to play chess in the wardrobe . . . to read Thackeray in the wings . . . to talk to your agent on the stage-door telephone . . . to act on a Sunday . . . to wear striped underwear . . ."?

Praying is important, particularly if it is directed to a particular saint. Saint Genesius is the most popular, for he is the patron saint of actors; he was an actor in the ancient theatres of Rome and was martyred by the Emperor Diocletian. Saint Christopher is another and so is Saint Cecilia, the patron saint of music. Derek Ayleward prays to Saint Anthony, an unusual choice. "I'm not a Catholic and I'm not even particularly religious, but I always say a prayer to Saint Anthony on first nights. He's the patron saint of lost property and supposing I lost my lines . . . ?" The prayers are usually muttered quickly and quietly in the wings just before the moment of entrance, but there are some very religious actors who will go down on their knees in the privacy of their dressing rooms and pray at length, Catholics will say a complete Rosary, Protestants will read from the Bible, and Jews will recite from the Talmud. But it must be remembered that good-luck rituals can be overdone and to be too crawlingly servile when asking favors from the lucky angels is bad luck, for it is likely to trigger off a very unwelcome streak of sadism. Before the opening of Noel Coward's play *Waiting in the Wings* in 1960, Marie Lohr went to Saint Mark's Church and prayed long and hard for a good first night. On the way to the theatre she slipped and broke her arm. "No good deed ever goes unpunished" was Coward's acid comment. Sir Alec Guinness remembers with a painful smile the night he played Hamlet for the Festival of Britain in 1951 at the New Theatre. An hour before he arrived at the theatre, he went round the Garrick Club, anxiously touching all the busts and portraits of Shakespeare for luck. One would have been enough, but to touch all three was definitely overdoing it. The production, opening cold without the benefit of a pre-London tour of previews (this was the dark ages before previews had been invented), was dismally under-rehearsed. A new switchboard had just been installed which played havoc with the complex lighting cues and effects. The company consisted of some of the most talented and distinguished actors then available, including the fledgling critic, Kenneth Tynan, making his first and only appearance on the professional stage as Player King, but the kiss of death was on the production and all managed to give the worst performances of their lives. And if all that wasn't enough, the public took a great and unreasonable hate to the beard which Guinness wore for the part, and, for the first and only time in his career, there were boos from the gallery at the end.

I myself once called in on a church on my way to the audition for a part which I very much wanted and appeased my excessive nerves by putting a pound note into the poor box and paying another pound for a candle. I arrived at the theatre glowing with high moral satisfaction and complacency, saying to myself, "Well, after all that, I've just *got* to get it." The audition was a terrible failure, and, not only did I not get the part, but I didn't work again for three months, so the only possible conclusion is that God, like the Metropolitan Police, doesn't take kindly to attempted bribery.

Continuity is important. Many actors, like John Moore, will always keep a prop from the previous play, an ashtray, a pencil, a pair of spectacles, a scarf. Some actors will always use an old set of makeup sticks on a first night and will never break into a new stick, bottle, or tube until the play has been running at least a week. Peter Barkworth takes this idea one stage further: he won't start a new tin of pancake at the beginning of a performance any night; he must wait until halfway through the evening, perhaps till after the interval. This distrust of newness extends to clothes: Richard Dennis will never wear an entirely new, freshly laundered shirt on a first night; it must have been worn once before at the dress rehearsal. Al Jolson always wore old clothes on his opening nights, and Jim Dale will never change a costume during a long run. If it wears out and has to be replaced, then a fragment of the original costume must somehow be incorporated in the new one. On the other hand, newness can bring good luck. Some actors, like Robert Selbie, regard it as lucky to wear something new on the first day of rehearsal, and there was once a certain eminent actress, luckily with a wealthy husband, who invariably bought a new piece of jewelry and wore it throughout the rehearsals of a new play. Before the war actors were expected to look like gentlemen and to dress smartly, but Laurence Olivier's habit of appearing on every day of the *Mary Queen of Scots* rehearsals in a different suit, aroused a certain jealous hostility from his colleagues. "Each suit is a relic of a different flop," was Olivier's prompt explanation, a remark which greatly endeared him to the company and started lifelong friendships which survive to this day.

All these superstitions are personal, but there are dozens of general ones which, in total defiance of logic or common sense, are regarded by the theatrical fraternity as Holy Writ. Their origins are lost in the mists of theatrical history and they cast an intriguing light on human gullibility. It's good luck if your shoes squeak on your first entrance, for this means the audience will love you; nobody has ever been able to explain why this is, but one old actress I knew in my early days in the theatre assured me that it was so and it had frequently happened to her. For this reason she always bought cheap shoes, as these were the only variety that could be relied on to squeak loudly enough.

If you get a first-night telegram then you must immediately destroy the envelope, and if you are writing a letter in connection with your work, you must get the stamp from a friend and not pay for it. This means you will get the job. It's very good luck to fall flat on your face when you make your entrance; the play will then be a huge success. There is one interesting example of this in the first production of *Dracula* at the Little Theatre, London, when an actor called Stuart Lomath tripped over the Gothic doorway and fell heavily onto the stage. Apparently the effect was more sinister than amusing, for the audience uttered a collective gasp of alarm instead of laughing, seeing in the incident yet another manifestation of Count Dracula's evil influence. Nobody had any faith in the play, and all were greatly surprised when it ran two years in London and a year in New York with a lucrative film deal to follow.

Finding a piece of cotton thread is good luck as long as it is either backstage or on the stage itself (dressing rooms don't count). This indicates a forthcoming contract with a producer whose initial corresponds with the number of times you can wind it round your finger. Once round means *A*, suggesting that Mr. Donald Albery will be requiring your services; three times round means *C*, indicating that it is Michael Codron, Ray Cooney, or the Festival Theatre at Chichester who will be fighting for you. Seven times would be *G*, for Gale, and if you were lucky enough to find a piece of thread long enough to wind round your finger thirteen times, as once did happen to a certain aged American actor, then Mr. David Merrick would be smiling in your direction. There is an alternative version of this which I heard from a music-hall lady ventriloquist (old enough to remember the days when such people were called *artistes* and no nonsense about it). You must take the thread from somebody's jacket or dress and drop it onto the ground, and if it fell into the shape of a letter that would be the initial of your next employer.

Leslie Banks was always intensely irritated by a certain actress who spent her time picking threads from his jacket and dropping them onto the floor whenever she played a scene with him. "The dandruff scraper and fluff twirler" he would peevishly describe her. He always wondered why she did it and this would now appear to be the explanation.

It is very bad luck to whistle in the dressing room or indeed anywhere inside the theatre, for that means that the play will be finishing soon. Those who really do believe in the darker side of the supernatural will explain that, by whistling, you are summoning the Devil. "Whistle and I'll come to you," runs the old Cornish saying. It is further believed that the one sitting nearest the door in the dressing room will get the sack. There would seem to be some truth in this, for in my first year in the theatre (1950), I was sacked from my first three jobs, the repertory companies at Watford, Bromley, and Darlington. I can remember that on all three occasions some actor in the dressing room had whistled only the day before and that my place at the long trestle table was nearest the door; this being the coldest and draftiest place is where the newcomer to the company traditionally sits. The first occasion had definitely been malice aforethought from an older actor I had unwittingly offended. The second and third were, I like to think, both accidents from actors as young and inexperienced as myself who presumably did not know any better. There is a simple, traditional way of canceling the bad luck: you must leave the dressing room, turn round three times, knock on the door, and then beg humbly to be readmitted. Profanity has a healthy neutralizing effect, and a stream of obscene words will quickly banish any evil spirit in hearing. In the stage area, whistling was exceedingly dangerous for a good commonsensical reason. In the eighteenth and nineteenth centuries the stage staff, who were responsible for the raising and lowering of the scenery, were recruited from the navy, for seamen understood how to handle the ropes on which the scenery was strung. They were traditionally directed by the stage manager who whistled at them, one for raise and two for lower. Any foolish actor or visitor whistling backstage could cause total confusion in the performance and could even get the scenery on his head.

Views on the supposedly bad luck of the number thirteen differ considerably within theatrical circles. For most people it is bad luck, as with Dudley Moore who, in a typically witty letter, said, "I'm not *really* superstitious, but if my play opened on Friday 13th and I found myself in No. 13 dressing-room on the 13th floor and the theatre was No. 13 in the street, then I might think that things were beginning to stack up on me." Jean Kent remembers how very distressed she and the company she was leading were when they were flown out to South Africa on Friday 13. Old actors used to say that if there are thirteen in the company, then three will get the sack. Eddie Cantor would rewrite his entire script if the original was thirteen pages long, and there are producers who will never open a play on the thirteenth of the month. One famous Edwardian theatrical lodging house in Brighton had a room number 13, but nobody would use it. The landlady tried to take off the jinx by redecorating it, putting in running water and room service (early-morning tea, an exotic luxury), but it was all useless. Nobody would touch it, and it was eventually turned into a bathroom. The number 13 has a sinister significance in the world of American TV series. They are planned in batches of thirteen and if one doesn't succeed in finding its audience, it is dropped after the thirteenth installment, as Diana Rigg found to her cost in her own series, "Diana." Pat Phoenix, much-loved star of "Coronation Street," which is coming near to breaking all world records for longevity, decided to leave the series after a financial dispute. She wanted an extra £100 a week and Granada TV would only offer her £20. Her departure and that of her husband, Alan Browning, who was also in the series, were loudly mourned by the fans, but her decision was made and she stuck to it. She had been with the series for thirteen years.

On the other hand, the number carries a reassuring amount of good luck for some people. It was Eric Portman's favorite lucky number, and it has been thought that play titles with thirteen letters are usually very lucky. A random selection of these would include *The Magistrate*, *The Profligate*, *The Wizard of Oz*, *The Silver King*, and *In Old Kentucky*. There is an interesting superstition connected with the number. On Broadway and in many other American cities, it is considered good luck to start the performance thirteen minutes late. This means a happy and responsive audience and a fine performance to match, for it is a sad and inescapable truth of theatrical life that if the audience is bad then the actors are unlikely to be good. There is a practical reason for this as with many superstitions, and it stems from the notorious un-punctuality of American theatregoers. No power of heaven and earth can persuade New Yorkers to get to the theatre on time, a phenomenon which is difficult to explain; for in view of the in-sane prices of the tickets, they might be expected to fall over backward rather than miss a single minute of the entertainment. Rather than torment the unhappy company with the nuisance of chattering, rattling latecomers, the curtain is held for thirteen minutes. It seems to work.

It is bad luck to speak the last line of the play (called the tag line) at rehearsal, though there are some subtle variations on this. Some say it applies only to a new play; others say that, old or new, it applies only to the dress rehearsal, though I have known old actors who refuse to say it at any time and could only with reluctance be persuaded to say it on the first night. Nobody has ever been quite sure why this is unlucky, but many a novice actor like myself who has innocently done so has been shot down in flames by the older actors in the company. One theory which has been tentatively advanced is this: if you don't say the tag line then this is one little thing which hasn't been rehearsed; this knowl-edge will be a tiny pinprick of worry, and this will produce an el-ement of tension in your first-night performance which is com-monly regarded as an essential ingredient of good acting. This is only a theory and not a very convincing one, because first nights are quite tense enough without going out of one's way to make them any worse. The other and much more plausible idea is that anything which is complete is tempting Providence, for the imp-ish humor of the Fates will bring them to destroy anything which is perfect, since perfection is the privilege only of the gods. This is why builders won't put in the last brick or shipbuilders the last rivet and why Michaelangelo left unpainted a tiny section of the ceiling in the Sistine Chapel. Some producers, particularly in the pantomime world, take this superstition very seriously, and Emile Littler would never allow his principals even to know what the tag line was until they came to the last scene, at which point a uniformed attendant would enter the stage and give it to them in a sealed envelope. Patrick Ludlow, who stage-managed a number of the postwar Littler pantomimes, has preserved a couple of these state secrets for posterity:

CINDERELLA: And now our evening work is done,
We hope you've all had lots of fun.

ROBIN HOOD: And that's the story of Robin Hood,
We know you'll come back to this wood.

Some producers go to what must surely be considered an unreasonable length to avoid trouble and will not allow the principal in question to speak the tag line even on the first night. The principal concerned must speak some gibberish in rhyme. June Grey remembers reciting,

ALADDIN: "di-dum, di-dum, di-dum, di-dum,
"Dumdidi, dum diddi, dumdiddi, *DUM!*"

greatly to the bewilderment of the audience, though the orchestra was also playing and thus partially covered the gap. Ellen Terry remembered a significant incident in her youth when she was playing Julia in *The Rivals*. During the rehearsals she faithfully observed the then centuries-old tradition by never speaking the tag line,

JULIA: But in judging passion will force the gaudier into the wreath whose thorn offends them when its leaves are dropped.

Exeunt omnes.

When the first performance came, the prompter heard this for the first time and was greatly confused to hear her say it with an upward inflection, which she later claimed made good sense, rather than the traditional downward inflection. An upward inflection implies that there is more to come, so the wretched man stood there with his hands on the curtain rope waiting for it. She recalled in her memoires that there was a terrible embarrassment while the company waited for the curtain to come down, and it wasn't until Mr. Buckstone as Bob Acres had shouted for all the audience to hear (he was very deaf), "What the devil does all this mean; why don't you bring the damned curtain down?" that the prompter did so.

A similar incident dogged a repertory production of *The Importance of Being Earnest* in the early fifties. The final two lines, just in case there is any reader who does not know them, are as follows:

LADY BRACKNELL: My nephew, you appear to be displaying signs of triviality.

WORTHING: On the contrary, Aunt Augusta, I have just discovered for the first time in my life the vital importance of being Earnest.

All embrace. Curtain.

The actor playing Ernest not only refused to speak his final line in the rehearsals but rashly assumed that all the backstage staff knew about the superstition. On the first night the young and inexperienced stage manager who did not, and rather more surprisingly did not know the final line of the play, brought down the curtain on Lady Bracknell's line, thereby robbing the leading man of his privilege of ending the play. When the combined wrath of the company fell on his head, he defended himself, not unreasonably, by explaining that he had thought Lady Bracknell's line to be the final one because at no time during rehearsals had he heard any other. Matheson Lang always liked to end his productions himself and, irrespective of the play or the part, would rewrite the final scene to give himself the tag line, but in rehearsal he would always substitute the words "Colleen Bawn" greatly to the bewilderment of the company's newcomers. These are only three examples of an accident which can be duplicated endlessly in theatrical history and which confirm one basic fact of life—that to leave anything unrehearsed, however trivial or apparently unimportant, is very dangerous.

Opening umbrellas on the stage doesn't seem to bother anybody in England, but in America there is a lot of bad luck associated with it. It started in 1868 when an orchestra leader named Bob Williams, saying good-bye to the company before going away for the weekend, opened his umbrella while standing on the stage, and walked out into a very rainy day. An hour later he was standing on the boat, waving good-bye to a party of friends. As it sailed away from the jetty, one of the engines exploded and Williams was killed instantly. In the resulting publicity it seemed that the accident and the open umbrella were connected and thus a new theatrical superstition was born. This then produced a rather bizarre little problem for producers, for although in the legitimate theatre the opening of an umbrella might well be avoided with a little judicious rearrangement of text and production, the twirling parasol, either singly or collectively, was always an essential ingredient of the late nineteenth-century musical stage. Rose Coghlan, a big musical star of the nineties, twirled her red parasol in *Fashion* at Wallacks Theatre with unmatched zest and skill but was severely criticized in a very ungentlemanly manner by the press for thus endangering the future success of the entertainment. It was Marie Tempest in her Broadway success *The Marriage of Kitty* who, with her usual cool, forthright, commonsensical way of organizing her life, decided that opening an umbrella or parasol on the stage was not unlucky provided you pointed it toward the floor and opened it downward, thus indicating that you had all your troubles under your feet. From then on, umbrellas were always opened downward, and Jeanne Eagels on the first night of *Rain* was reminded of this in a first-night telegram. She went on to score the greatest success of her career.

Peacocks in any form—feathers or fans or peacock designs on the stage—are very unlucky. There will be trouble and not the least from mutinous principals. Oscar Asche had all the peacock fans destroyed at the dress rehearsal of *Chu Chin Chow* which then proceeded to break all existing records with a run of five years.

Jeanne Eagels was warned by a first-night telegram about managing her parasol in Rain.

Tom Walls would go berserk if any importunate designer tried to sneak peacock patterns into the setting of the Aldwych farces, and there is an intriguing story about Sir Henry Irving playing Othello to Edwin Booth's Iago at the Lyceum Theatre in the 1880s.

Booth, who had sharp eyes, reported to Irving (who was very shortsighted) in the intermission that there was a woman in the front row of the stalls who had a large peacock fan. Irving became greatly agitated and sent a letter to her by one of the attendants. It said: "For God's sake, take your peacock's fan out of the theatre to avoid disaster!" The woman, anxious to obey, handed it to the attendant for disposal who, terrified, refused to take it. Eventually the woman left the theatre herself and threw it into a nearby dustbin. Unfortunately it was too late to save the evening from disaster, for Irving's Othello was one of the few complete failures in his long and glorious career, and after the brief engagement, he never played it again. Booth had good reason to dread the peacock. When he built his huge and splendid theatre on Sixth Avenue, New York, in the 1870s, a close friend gave him a magnificent stuffed peacock. Booth was very reluctant to hurt his friend's feelings; he accepted it with a convincing show of gratitude and placed it in the front lobby. The theatre and his management were a failure. One disastrous production followed another, and within a couple of years he was bankrupt. In later years he not only quarreled violently with his so-called friend when doubting his benevolence, but also attributed the downfall of his managerial ambitions to "that miserable bird of malignant fate!" His unhappy experience would seem to have gone unheeded by other managers, for when the Bijou Theatre was built in 1892, a dado of peacock feathers was painted round the auditorium. Once again bad luck hit the theatre, with one failure after another. Soon the word circulated that it was an unlucky theatre, and it wasn't until some years later that the dado was repainted a cheerful blue and the theatre enjoyed its first success with a light comedy *Midnight Belle*. From then it became one of New York's luckiest theatres.

Then there are some unlucky colors. Yellow is bad luck because this is the color worn by the Devil in the medieval mystery plays. Yellow roses in a bouquet mean the death of an old friend, and a yellow dog in a play means a death in the company. Yellow clarinets are considered unlucky in America, and, though they have vanished completely from the theatre world, they were once in common use in orchestra pits. Nat Goodwin, the vaudeville comedian, would go berserk if he saw one and would threaten to walk out if the offending musician did not take his instrument away. Black is unlucky because of its old association with death, and many people will refuse to wear it on the stage. There was a time when actors would get their dinner jackets, tails, and dress trousers made of midnight blue instead of black; it looked like black under the lights and was considered exceedingly smart.

But the unluckiest color of all is undoubtedly green. You must not wear it, nor must you have it on the stage or in anything connected with the play. There are a number of ingenious explanations for this: one is that it dates back to the days when stages had green cloths on the floor or when actors invariably performed out-of-doors on green lawns (hence the old actor's expression, "see you on the green"). So if an actor was wearing green while standing on something green, he would not be properly visible. The other theory puts it down to the traditional green spotlight which illuminated the eighteenth and nineteenth centuries' leading actors. It was known as the "lime" (hence the *limelight*) and was particularly popular for illuminating the villains in old-time melodramas. So if you were foolish enough to wear green while bathed in a green spotlight, the two colors would cancel each other out.

Witches and those involved in the occult profession explain it very simply. Green is the fairies' own special color, and they are jealous and hostile if mere mortals wear it, even if the mortal in question is impersonating a fairy. But there is a very practical explanation for green's unpopularity and that is the problem it gives to theatre electricians and designers; Michael Sinclair, an English actor and stage manager now living in New York, sums it up tersely: "Green is a real bitch to light; it always looks like muddy brown." But whatever the reason, people will go out of their way to avoid green. One West End producer will not allow it on stage or in any company he employs. Even the two male actors' volumes of *Spotlight*, inescapable to any theatrical organization, are banished to his outer office where he can't see them because of the two strips of green on the cover. Michael Codron admits quite cheerfully that he believes in this superstition and further to being a mass of "unformulated and illogical belief." He states that one evening during the run of *There's a Girl in My Soup*, he discovered that the set was predominantly green, there were green books on the shelves, and that the poster advertising was green. He is now cautiously reconciled to the color because the play had at that point been running for two years which by any standards can be called successful. But I remember an actress of considerable antiquity in my early days who found herself rehearsing on a green carpet, was given a script with a green cover, and a green shawl to wear, and her first line was "my dear how beautiful you are, I'm positively green with jealousy." She lost her voice, had to be replaced, left the theatre cursing the color and convinced that this had been the source of her troubles.

On the other hand, the theatrical fraternity has always been happily reconciled to the communal sitting room backstage being called the Greenroom, and there is in London a well-known and very prosperous actors' club of that name. Green writing paper appears to be lucky, and it's interesting to note that George Bernard Shaw invariably wrote his famous letters on paper of this color, saying that it was restful to his eyes. These letters found their way to many dressing-room tables, particularly those of Ellen Terry and Mrs. Patrick Campbell, and few playwrights enjoyed such an unbroken string of successes as Shaw did between 1900 and 1932. I invariably used green notepaper embossed with Shaw's address in Whitehall Court when impersonating him in *Dear Liar* and *The First Night of Pygmalion*, and both of these plays have been very lucky for me. Play titles with the word green are also blessed with luck, *Green Julia*, *Green for Danger*, *The Corn Is Green*, *How Green Was My Valley*, *The Green Bay Tree*, *The Green Goddess*, and *The Green Pastures*, to name only seven which spring instantly to mind. *The Green Pastures* provides an interesting footnote to this inquiry. Its success in the thirties on Broadway and round the American continent was legendary, but the aura was slightly tarnished by a series of unaccountable and sinister deaths. Wesley Hill, the actor playing the Archangel Gabriel, was killed by a passing taxi. Sam Davies, his successor in the part, died of a heart attack. The third actor in the part committed suicide. By now the company was getting worried. Clearly there was a jinx somewhere, but why? Was it the part and if not, then what was it? It was finally suggested by one of the company who had a knowledge of witchcraft that the curse was not on the part but on the horn which Gabriel has to play in De Lawd's office, the horn having a rather sinister significance in certain forms of voodoo. Thus reassured, the fourth actor, Orlando Jeffs, consented to play the part but not the horn, and thus a superstition was born which has survived till the present day. In the film version (1935), Oscar Polk insisted on following the tradition and the scene was tactfully rewritten. Gabriel picks up the horn, looks sadly at it, puts it to his mouth silently, and then replaces it on De Lawd's desk, saying rather guiltily as De Lawd enters, "Ahm jest itchin' to blow one good toot on dat horn, Lawd." De Lawd smiles gently, and Gabriel pulls away the horn which is never seen or referred to again.

Old actors consider it very bad luck to have a tin trunk while on tour; it must be leather or one of those spacious wicker baskets known in the profession as skips. Tin trunks are unlucky because they resemble coffins, and anything which even remotely resembles or reminds you of death is to be avoided. For this reason you must never have a real coffin on the stage and if the play—as with *Loot* or *Richard III*—requires one you must never hire it from a local undertaker; it must be specially constructed in the theatre workshop. A camelback trunk, which is one with a rounded top, is considered unlucky in America. They are difficult to pack in baggage cars, and in the old touring days many managers refused to allow them. Any young hopeful thus encumbered would be given the choice of either dismissal or being forced to replace it very expensively with one of conventional shape. Likewise, a corded trunk is bad luck because the cord represents the hangman's rope and thus the company will be hanged with bad notices. Ethel Barrymore once in her very early days traveled with a corded trunk and was sternly ordered by the company manager to uncord it immediately and substitute leather straps. But it's good luck to have dozens of traveling labels pasted all over the trunk, for this is evidence of prosperity and experience and will thus get more respectful treatment from the porters and carriers.

Anything associated with death must naturally be avoided, and there was an interesting example of this in 1950 during the run of *His Excellency*. Owen Fellowes, playing a Middle Eastern prime minister, was involved in a very unpleasant accident in the underground. He fell onto the rails, his legs were amputated by a passing train, and he died shortly afterward in the hospital. His replacement, Richard Littledale, moved into the empty dressing room and wore his suit; shortly afterward, he died from gas poisoning. With two fatalities so close to each other of two actors playing the same part, the company was getting worried. The part, the dressing room, the suit, and the props were all clearly unlucky, and so the third actor, Walter Horseborough, was strongly advised to keep away from the fatal dressing room and not to use the suit or the props. He took the advice, and played the role successfully and without incident for the remainder of its two-year run.

The Spanish theatre takes quite a different view of death—in Spain they love it, they are obsessed with it, and this colors all their art. What the Spanish public likes about the plays and acting is the presence of death and this is how they judge them. *Con*

*Ethel Barrymore with two Russian wolfhounds who added authentic
color to the garden fête scene in* Rasputin and the Empress

fuende, meaning *with death,* is the highest praise they can bestow on a play or a performance. The plays of Lope de Vega and Lorca can be understood and appreciated only in the light of this.

It is very ironic that when the whole point and purpose of an actor's art is to produce an illusion of reality that the actual reality should be so carefully avoided. It's bad luck to have real money and real jewels on the stage. Apart from the obvious danger that they might be stolen, there is the strange paradox that real jewels never look real. From a distance they look small and colorless, and a competent property master with a supply of colored glass and tin can outshine a whole shop window of Cartier and Fabergé. Gertrude Lawrence took this superstition so seriously that when Douglas Fairbanks, Sr., in a gesture of well-meaning generosity, substituted real diamonds for the paste ones she wore during the run of *Private Lives* in 1930, she threw them into his face and reportedly refused ever to speak to him again.

Real antiques are bad for the same reason, for they never look entirely authentic no matter how splendid is their reality. A good illustration of this is the story of Sir Herbert Beerbohm Tree when he was asked to give a special Royal Gala performance of his Hamlet as part of the 1911 Coronation festivities and decided that to suit the occasion he would use in the play not the usual painted cardboard goblets but a set of antique medieval chalices made of gold and liberally studded with rubies, diamonds, and sapphires. They were borrowed from the British Museum at enormous cost and trouble. The insurance against loss, the deposit, the police escort to, during, and from the play added enormously to the costs of the operation, but the resultant publicity provided some compensation—Sir Herbert, in fur-lined coat and top hat, formally receiving the goblets (which did, it must be admitted, look marvelous) flanked by uniformed police constables, Sir Herbert supervising their unwrapping in his dressing room, Sir Herbert stating to the press that "nothing is too good for His Majesty and His Majesty's Theatre," and finally Sir Herbert (aged fifty-eight but who cared?) in his Hamlet costume, holding up one of the goblets and soliloquizing soulfully over it. The sad result of all this extravagance was a complaint from the *Times* critic, who had clearly not heard of all the fuss, that it was a great pity that the otherwise excellent production should have been spoiled by the use of goblets which were so obviously faked.

Real food is unlucky on the stage and there are some very hidebound old actors who will bluntly refuse to eat it. The tradition is that it must be fabricated to resemble real food but must not be what it is supposed to be. On the other hand it must be edible, since it does have to be eaten. Actors are very long-suffering and in the interests of our art we will eat and drink some unusually revolting things. As an unpaid student assistant stage manager at the Palace Theatre, Watford, in 1950 my duties during my first week included preparing a full breakfast for the first act of a tasteless farce of unusual ineptitude entitled *The Maiden's Prayer.* The meal which the unhappy actors were forced to eat with every appearance of enthusiasm consisted of strips of bread coated with gravy browning to represent bacon, circles of bread colored red to represent a tomato, and further circles of bread with a dab of mustard in the middle to look like a fried egg. The coffee was more diluted gravy browning (a very useful and ubiquitous commodity backstage), and the whiskey was cold tea. You could always rely on there being somebody in the stage box with a pair of binoculars, so the food had to look convincing. Preparing all this for six was a long and cumbersome task, and one day I asked innocently why we couldn't use the real thing which, I pointed out, would be much easier to prepare and would have the added advantage of being pleasanter to eat. "Quite impossible," said my immediate superior, a young acting stage manager named Michael Wynne. "You'd have to cook it just before it's needed and you're busy elsewhere. Those bastard electricians would nick the lot if they could, and anyway Wilkie wouldn't stand for it!" Wilkie or Harold J. Wilkinson was our resident old actor-laddie and a vintage example of his breed, it was from him that I learned

Marlow's *Dr. Faustus* was enlivened by the appearance on the stage of the six devils as specified by the author, but when the actor playing Faustus turned to count them, there were seven. He thought the seventh was a reflection in a mirror but it wasn't; it was the Devil himself who had chosen that moment to enter the stage. The audience ran out screaming, and the actor playing Faustus died of a heart attack.

It's bad luck to have a real Bible on the stage, for this is disrespectful to God; it must be an ordinary book painted to look like a Bible. It is unlucky to make the sign of the cross from left to right—it must be from right to left in the Greek Orthodox manner. The usual way is regarded as a mild form of blasphemy and will surely bring down holy wrath from somewhere up above, as many hundreds of actresses impersonating nuns in the various productions of *The Sound of Music* were taught. On this point, a number of interesting regional differences are to be found. In Ireland the superstition about the sign of the cross also applies to a number of pious objects, as I found to my cost. In 1962 I played a singing bishop in a musical called *Fursey* which starred Dublin's darling, the irrepressible and inimitable Milo O'Shea. Among the holy relics I wore was a pectoral cross. It was authentic, purchased in Rome, blessed by the Pope, and correct in every detail. A howl of anger rose from the Catholic pressure groups. There were many of them, they kept a watchful eye on the Dublin theatre, they wielded a terrifying power and influence, and they combined to denounce the use of a real pectoral cross as a terrible and dangerous blasphemy. A moan of anguish likewise rose from the company who swore it would bring bad luck not only to me but to them, to the show, and to the whole of the Dublin Theatre Festival of which *Fursey* was a proud and glittering centerpiece. With a stubbornness and determination worthy of a better cause, I refused to accept this nonsense and accordingly paid a visit to the head of the Catholic Church in Ireland, Archbishop Macquoid known, none too affectionately, as John Charles. I received an assurance that the pectoral cross was *not* offensive and triumphantly passed this on to the producer of the play who received the information very coldly.

"I don't give a damn for the archbishop" he said angrily. "It's the fockn Legion of Mary you've got to watch out for because they don't give a damn for him either." If I went ahead and wore the pectoral cross in defiance, then the Legion of Mary would picket the theatre. There would be riots, a lot of adverse publicity, and the show, whose decor he had himself designed and in which he had invested so much money, would be ruined. This threat was a very real one, so I then produced a substitute which had been mocked up in the Gaiety Theatre property room; it was a piece of cross-shaped tin studded with little beads of glass and suspended from a length of lavatory chain. But this was not acceptable either.

"Sure, it may not *be* real but it *looks* real, and that's just as bad!" I was told by the director, Alan Simpson. A compromise was eventually reached; I was allowed to wear a highly polished horse brass on a chain which might, at a distance, pass for a saintly medallion. This rather peculiar solution satisfied everybody, including the dreaded Legion of Mary.

There are a number of curious superstitions relating to the dressing room and the use of makeup. Whereas some always use old makeup sticks on first nights, there are others who will always arrange to have a completely new set in times of crisis and will go to considerable expense to get it. This may be due to an ancient story of revenge. A needle was inserted down the center of the stick and the enemy—all unsuspecting—would rip his face to pieces as he made himself up. Some consider it good luck to arrange the accessories on the left, hand mirror on the right, and the Leichner sticks arranged in a fan shape in the center.

But most actors, after a few years in the profession, regard it as good luck to use an old cigar box and to keep everything in it in rather an untidy, haphazard manner. It is quietly believed that only amateurs and enthusiastic beginners are religiously clean and tidy in the dressing room, and no actor wants to be thought a beginner. Only beginners sport those expensive Leichner metal makeup boxes with separate sections for each stick and sliding trays inside for the accessories, usually the present from a proud parent at the beginning of a career. A touch of elegant untidiness and artistic sleaziness inspires confidence in your age, expertise, and experience. In fact I know one old actor-laddie who boasts proudly that he hasn't cleaned or even tidied his makeup box for thirty-seven years.

Some actors consider it bad luck to unpack the makeup box until after the first night and the notices, for better or worse, are out. Sascha von Scherler, the American actress, never unpacks her box until the end of the first week. To unpack any earlier indicates a smug assumption that you will be in residence for a long time, and the angels of luck are quick to punish complacency. This practice is commonly observed in the American theatre and is thought to have originated with Booth. There are, in addition, some old actors who consider it rather good luck to piss into the dressing-room basin and don't consider that a young actor can truly call himself a professional until he has performed this rather distasteful ceremony of initiation.

Chorus girls believe that it's bad luck to spill powder on the floor, but if you stamp and dance on it, then you will very quickly become a star. It is not known whether or not this ever actually happened, but the belief survives strongly. If you drop a pair of scissors on the ground, you must always get somebody else to pick them up. It's bad luck to look over another actor's shoulder into his section of the dressing-room mirror, for this has associations with the evil eye, and the reason why so many actors carry hand mirrors for making up is due to the shortage of full-size mirrors in some of the more primitive theatres on tour. To break a mirror in a dressing room is dreadfully unlucky and will result in seven years bad luck. I have known a very nervous actress of some distinction refuse to dress in a room where a mirror had been broken.

Sometimes superstitions cancel each other out, since there are irreconcilable views as to their function and purpose. Suppose you stumble as you enter the stage. Some say this is good luck, some say it is bad. The reader must take his choice. Supposing you go to a strange producer's office for an interview and by mistake you go into the wrong door, an easy thing to do, especially in America where a single corridor in an office block will house a dozen producers whose offices are not always easily identified? Some say that this is good and you will get the part, some say it is bad and that you'll never work for him. Once again the reader must take his choice. Then there is the peculiar superstition about soap in the dressing room. Everybody agrees that it represents good luck, but should you take it with you on tour or should you leave it behind? Some old actors say you must leave it behind if you wish to return to the same theatre in the future. Others say with equal firmness that you must take it with you if you wish to enjoy good notices and a return engagement with the same management. The obvious solution would appear to be to have two cakes of soap, one to leave behind and one to take with you, and it is surprising that nobody has thought of this simple solution before. But perhaps the angels of luck don't take kindly to those clever people who hedge their bets.

Telegrams are another source of dissent. Some actors keep their first-night telegrams and cards and hopefully watch them grow dustier and yellower as the months and years flick by. Others say that this is bad luck and that they must be destroyed after the opening. Some actors keep one telegram for their next play, another example of how important continuity is in people's lives, whereas some believe continuity to be a bad thing and will always destroy something in their dressing room on the last night—it might be a light bulb, a plate, or an ashtray—as a gesture of absolute finality which is thought to prevent any evil impulse or spirit from following them into his next play.

You mustn't look through the gap in the front curtains to watch the audience coming in as this means curtains for the play. It is also regarded as unspeakably amateurish, the only insult you can throw at an actor which really hurts. For the same reason it's unlucky to lower the front curtain at the end of the dress rehearsal. This would be regarded as a symbolic gesture of finality which would result in a bad opening and a short run. But some actors always touch the curtain when it has finally come down. The curtain in some mysterious way represents good luck, and if you touch it then you will get good notices. The 1940 film, *Yankee Doodle Dandy*, starring James Cagney as George M. Cohan, was correct on this small point and did, in fact, give a very authentic picture of the sleazier side of vaudeville in the nineties.

If a star replaces another during a long run, it's very bad luck as well as bad manners for the incoming star to see the outgoing star's final performance, or to see it at all once the take-over has been decided. And it is equally bad luck and bad manners for the outgoing star to see the incoming star's first performance, nor must a good-luck telegram be sent. Instead a message must be scrawled on the dressing-table mirror with a stick of Leichner No. 5, this being a light creamy color and most visible on the surface.

Many superstitions go in threes. If one actor gets the sack then two more will follow. If you get one engagement at the Theatre Royal, Drury Lane (the luckiest of all the theatres), then you will get three. If you get a job offered, two more will be offered within the week. If you have one successful play then you'll have three in a row. In America it is believed that the best people go in threes: the three Barrymores, the three Frohmanns (David, Charles, and Guy, all producers), the three Sirens, three Slocums, three Whitstucks, all comedy trios from vaudeville. But old actors have traditionally been cautious about joining a company with three women, for it is believed that when two women get together they always talk and gossip about the third. This makes trouble and is very bad for the company's morale and inevitably their performances. Failure can also go in threes. Noel Coward always denied that he was in any way superstitious, but even he had to admit that there were definitely sinister elements at work when he had three flops in quick succession—*This Was a Man, Home Chat,* and *Sirocco,* all within four months. The young Laurence Olivier had no less than six failures in one year, 1929, and it was only his appearance in the uniquely successful *Private Lives* immediately afterward that reassured him that there was no jinx on his career.

The ritual of good-luck wishes on first nights is fraught with superstitious distaste and it is getting worse within our lifetime. To wish good luck to another person, so they say, is to part with it yourself. It also means that you are inviting the hostile and rather contemptuous intervention of the gods if you draw attention to your desperate need for fortune. I knew one neurotic actor who would go quietly berserk if anybody wished him good luck, or sent a telegram, or tried to give him a first-night present. He would creep on stage by a back staircase and skulk in the darkness of the wings until his entrance, avoiding like the plague meeting or even seeing anybody on the way.

In recent years a curious and rather repulsive tradition borrowed from the Continent has grown up of offering gruesome first-night wishes like "break a leg" or "fall down backward" or "give them hell" or "go and perform an impossible action" or just a stream of good-natured obscenities. But usually actors say pleasant, encouraging things like "be brilliant" or "enjoy yourself" or "have a marvelous time." A popular greeting much quoted by wits is Dorothy Parker's famous telegram to Uta Hagen, "a hand on your opening and may your parts grow bigger," and in America "knock them for a loop" has gained a wide currency.

Among the older actors a popular greeting was "skin off your nose" and this according to Tenniel Evans has a special significance. It apparently referred to the bad old days, before Mr. Leichner came to our rescue, when makeup was crude, coarse, and untested and when applied it invariably had a disastrous effect on the skin which started to peel off in patches. This is why the actors in the early part of the nineteenth century could always be identified by their blotchy complexions. So if you said "skin off your nose," you were in effect hoping that the actor would be in a position where he must continue to apply his makeup; in other words, to be in work, and that is the best wish you can extend to any actor.

Nowadays, good wishes are extended at dress rehearsals and this leads to another curious superstition, that it is good luck to have a bad dress rehearsal, as this means that the first performance will be good. Contrariwise, it is bad luck if the dress rehearsal is good, as this means a bad opening. I doubt if there is an actor in the theatre who hasn't experienced the forbidding truth of this. Good dress rehearsals are likely to make the company complacent and lazy and leads them to underrate the strain and difficulties of the actual first performance. If they have been acting up at a high dynamic level, they won't have enough energy left for the first night and the performance will suffer accordingly. It must be stated very firmly that the dress rehearsal mustn't be too bad, for total disaster merely makes everybody very angry and despair fills actors with a careless death wish. A dress rehearsal that is tense, nervy, strained with a few technical hitches and lapses of memory is acceptable. Of course in recent years the excellent custom of previews which started in New York and has happily spread to London has gone a long way to taking the edge off a first performance. Still an opening is an opening no matter how many weeks of previews you have, but at least they are now marginally less miserable.

Cats are traditionally the object of superstitious awe, both good and bad. Inside a theatre they usually represent good luck and are spoiled and cherished by the actors and stage staff, led firmly by the wardrobe mistress whose room provides a warm and comfortable home. If it takes an interest in the rehearsals and watches from the wings, then this is lucky, but if it strays onto the stage or, worse still, actually crosses it, then this is very bad. One hysterical actress to my certain knowledge refused to work all that day when it happened. But if it makes a mess in the dressing room, then this is the luckiest event of all. This very thing happened to Noel Coward on the first night of *The Vortex* in London. It was just before the curtain and everybody assured him that it was a lucky omen. He was paralyzed with nerves and refused to cheer up, stating that it was a very sensible comment on the whole play. *The Vortex* was a triumphant success and set its youthful author on the way to true stardom, so perhaps there's something in it. If this little accident happens during a performance, then the result is obviously going to be disastrous, for animals and children are traditional show stealers. Rachel was such a victim. Her death scene in *Judith* was one of the greatest experiences the Comedie Française offered its patrons. One night a black cat walked on the stage and left its candid comment on the floor. It stopped the play and reduced the audience to hysterical laughter, but what Rachel did not know was that it had been lured onto the stage by a rival tragedienne in the company.

Superstitions are not confined to the stage and the dressing room. They are to be found in the managerial offices and even in that little temple of hardheaded materialism, the box office. Box-office managers believe that if a queue is outside the window after a successful first night and the first person pays with a torn banknote, this is unlucky and the play will be off within a week. But if the first person is an old man, then the play will run for a year. "What happens if the old man at the head of the queue pays with a torn banknote?" I asked my informant. "It did happen," he smiled, and the Fates neatly split the difference. We ran exactly six months." Producers have good reason to be nervous, since the financial risks they habitually run are considerable. Some will open their plays on a Tuesday or an even-numbered day. Some will never open on a Friday or an odd-numbered day. Some producers regard it as good luck to open after a flop because the critics, having vented their spleen, will probably be more kindly disposed. Some producers will never give free tickets to a cross-eyed man or to a woman.

Usherettes have their own pet superstitions, particularly relating to the number thirteen. If the first person in the audience sits in row M, which is the thirteenth row, then it will be a bad evening with a loss of tips and plenty of worry and aggravation. If a woman tries to tip them, this is frequently regarded as bad luck and many usherettes won't accept it. If anybody actually sits in the thirteenth seat in a row, this is regarded as potential trouble and a watchful eye is kept on the occupant. It's bad luck if a woman faints in the theatre and if a woman, instead of her male escort, buys a program. It's bad luck if the usherette doesn't hear the first line of the play, and this accounts for the fact, noted by many patrons, that when the curtain rises, the usherette will momentarily stop whatever she is doing and listen intently. These worthy women believe that if they make a mistake about seating somebody, then they will make two more before the evening is finished. They further believe that the first tip of the play's run on the first night is lucky and must be rubbed against the leg. After that it must be kept permanently in the pocket for the rest of the play's run as a coaxer, a spur to fate. It's bad luck if the first customer in the theatre has a complimentary ticket. The first ticket must be bought and paid for or there will be more comps than money in the house thereafter. Some producers believe that it is bad luck for the show if the first customer is a woman, and there is record of a rather misogynic gentleman trying to prevent a lady from entering until a man arrived to save the situation. William Wheatley, manager of the Niblo Garden Theatre in New York used to employ a man to stand and wait in the lobby especially to avoid this disaster.

Some producers are superstitious about titles. *Three Blind Mice* is known to be an unlucky title, though nobody knows why. Christopher Fry was going to use it for one of his early plays but was persuaded to change it. Agatha Christie used this title for one of her crime plays in the early fifties and sent it to Peter Saunders who promptly changed it—not, he firmly maintains—because it was unlucky, but because there was already a play with that title. Whatever the reason, it turned out to be a very lucky decision, because the new title was *The Mouse Trap* which is currently in its twenty-third record-breaking year and has made an immense fortune for all concerned. Miracle in the title is unlucky and few plays with it have ever succeeded. Peacock is unlucky for the reasons already stated, and its presence in a title prophesies real trouble. Peter Bull lost a lot of money over Noel Langley's *Cage Me a Peacock*, Anouilh's *Cry of a Peacock* was a failure both in London and Paris, and *Juno and the Paycock*, though rightly regarded as a classic masterpiece, has never enjoyed a long run nor has it made money. It remains obstinately a great play which everybody admires but only a few actually want to see. Two popular words whose presence in the title is a fair guarantee of success are sex and murder. It is thought that T. S. Eliot had a shrewd awareness of the latter when his play about St. Thomas à Becket was named, not after the hero as might be expected, but *Murder in the Cathedral*. Admittedly many of the people who flock to see it do so in the happy expectation of seeing yet another crime drama by the indefatigable Agatha Christie (confusing it, doubtless, with her immensely popular *Murder in the Vicarage*), but flock they do, not once but many times. As Shaw perceptively commented, there is a strong vein of the purest masochism in the English public, and anybody who can bore them stiff in the interests of culture can reap huge profits.

A singularly death-wishing title in England was a musical originally called *Give Me the Bird*, the brainchild of two Americans who hopefully launched it in London with Gladys Cooper making her first and only appearance in the treacherous field of musical comedy. She pointed out to the authors what they clearly did not know, that in English theatre slang, getting the bird means being booed off the stage, and to title a play thus was literally to ask for trouble. Reluctantly, they consented to change it to *The Crystal Heart* but it didn't make any difference. Gladys Coo-

per had a solitary number in the show from which the title had
been taken. The words, and I quote from memory, were:

> Give me that bird,
> Where is that bird?
> Oh *give* me that bird
> that maddening—
> —saddening—
> —gladdening—
> BIRD!

It was too much. The gallery, which had been very patient
while ineptitude and triteness burst like an avalanche of yester-
day's porridge over the stalls, finally screamed out their contempt
and anger. And that was the end of *The Crystal Heart*, though it
struggled on to empty houses for a full month.

In France, the unlucky word is *ficelle*, meaning string. It must
never be used in a title, nor in the dialogue of a play, nor must it
be mentioned backstage or anywhere inside the theatre. If the
context of the play makes it necessary, then the word *corde* must
be used instead.

In America the unlucky words are bomb and turkey. How
curious that bomb should mean opposite things on two sides of
the Atlantic, for in England bomb means success, as in the
phrase, "It went like a bomb, old boy," which one actor could
well use to another in the dressing room while the cheers of the
first-night audience are still echoing round the theatre.* This is
yet another example of Bernard Shaw's famous saying that England and America are two countries separated by a common language.

As for turkey, the all-time record for the shortest Broadway
run is unarguably held by a drama called *Cage Me a Turkey*. The

* The one place where this phrase was never used—by general agreement
among the theatrical fraternity—was in Belfast during its years of civil
war. During this explosive period the expression did come painfully near
the truth.

play was about, and performed by, a group of dwarfs whose talent and experience of the theatre was, to put it very diplomatically, limited, and among the decorations prominently displayed in the drawing-room set was a stuffed turkey and a stuffed peacock. Many plays finish after the first performance, there is no longer any novelty in that, but *Cage Me a Turkey* has made a tiny footnote in history by failing to finish after the first. It seemed that a violent argument broke out among the company during the intermission. Some of them ended up in the hospital, and the audience had to leave the theatre without seeing the final act. But the most self-destroying title in American theatre history was a wartime play produced in 1967 called *We Bombed in New Haven*. New Haven is one of those indispensable places on a pre-Broadway tour whose audiences are notoriously difficult to please and which is known as a theatrical graveyard where the bones of countless Broadway shows lie rotting in the autumn sun. *We Bombed in New Haven* didn't quite do what its title promised. It did manage to reach Broadway but unhappily it didn't stay long.

Closing in New Haven was one of the occupational hazards of the American touring theatre to which all actors were resigned but there were many others. For fifty years, between roughly 1880 and 1930, America was covered with a vast network of touring theatres of formidable complexity. It kept thousands of actors in perpetual employment and kept its multimillion audience happily entertained before the talking cinema killed it. The scruffier side of touring life is shown with praiseworthy accuracy in the silent film *Exit Smiling*, which gave Beatrice Lillie her first and greatest starring part and which, in addition, contrives to be as excruciatingly funny as the best of Chaplin and Keaton. This rather specialized theatrical life stimulated and accumulated a series of rather unusual superstitions.

Sunday rehearsals were bad luck: it meant that a death would occur in the company and that the salaries would not be paid. This last was possibly the more intimidating threat, for being stranded and penniless in some remote outpost of the country was every touring actor's favorite nightmare. Unhappily it still is, for even in this day and age of easy communications and Equity it can happen, as with the unhappy group of English and American actors recently given eighteen-month contracts at a generous salary with a company in New Zealand. They discovered, when they arrived there, that the company had gone bankrupt and their salaries, contrary to managerial assurances, had not been deposited. Sunday rehearsals in America did take their toll and a number of victims are on record; Millie Cavendish, famous soubrette of the musical theatre in the nineties, was compelled to rehearse for three successive Sundays in a play called *The Crook* and died of a heart attack on the fourth. The play did open, and closed immediately. Jim Fisk, manager of the Grand Opera House in Chicago, had a rather more melodramatic ending as befitted the melodrama he was rehearsing. Not only did he rehearse on a Sunday, but he also even enforced performances on a Sunday which actors have always hated: in New York they are now an accepted part of the theatre scene, but actors in England have so far been mercifully spared them. Jim Fisk was shot dead by gangsters, and the play was swiftly withdrawn, having lost a fortune for all concerned. Fisk's death was generally regarded by the religious pressure groups as a highly fitting punishment for his blasphemy. But with a total lack of logic, it was said to be good luck to sign a contract on a Sunday.

If a train carrying the company arrives at a station with a graveyard on the right that was good luck; if it was on the left, that was bad luck and the performance that evening would be a bad one. An old actor's poem neatly sums up the situation:

> Graveyard on right
> Good house tonight.
> Graveyard to the left
> House will be bereft.

It was shockingly bad luck to have a corpse on the train, and

there are records of companies bluntly refusing to travel with
such a neighbor and their touring schedule had to be drastically
revised. One hunchback in the company is good luck but two are
bad. It is not known, though, what sort of luck is produced by
three hunchbacks.

Certain tunes were unlucky: "Home Sweet Home" and "Marriage Bells" are bad and indicate the early closing of the play.
Anybody heard singing them either in the theatre or in their lodgings or even on the train would be dismissed instantly. After 1912
and the *Titanic* disaster (whose victims included Charles Froh-
man), "Nearer My God to Thee" was added to the list. Once
again it can be seen that anything remotely connected with death
acquires bad luck and must be carefully avoided. This accounts
for the striking absence from the American scene of a hugely popular comedy, *Our American Cousin*, which was the play Lincoln
was watching on the night of his death.

When a touring company arrived in a town, it was the custom
to parade through the streets on a cart or coach, in costume, dancing, singing, distributing leaflets and thus publicizing that evening's performance. If a hay cart passed on this royal progress,
this was good luck. But if you saw a funeral procession coming
toward you, then it was essential to go down a side street and wait
till it went by, for never under any circumstances must you allow
a corpse to pass you. If there was no side street, then the parade
must disband temporarily, the cart drawn in to the side, and the
company must turn their backs to the street, since even to look on
death was bad luck. It was bad luck to see the full moon through
glass but good luck to sign a contract under moonlight. But would
it be very cynical to wonder which parsimonious, pleasure-killing
landlady managed to convince her lodgers that prunes for dinner
represented good luck provided they were all eaten, and that failure to do so meant a bad house and loss of receipts?

Poverty and hardship, cheerfully and unresentfully accepted,
were the lot of most of the profession, and particularly the blacks.
The Green Pastures and *Porgy and Bess* gave them a new lease on life

and self-respect, but until then their professional careers were exceedingly hard and artistically frustrating. Comic and servile stereotypes were the order of the day and not many of those. Hardship breeds determination and determination breeds hope and thus a whole series of minor but intriguing superstitions grew up among the theatrical blacks. It was bad luck to applaud any number at rehearsal, for it meant that it would be cut at a later stage or fail dismally on the first night and thus be cut later. It was bad luck to count the audience if it was scattered sparsely over the house unless it could be done so discreetly that nobody could see it. It was bad luck when the actors came to the theatre to ask them if they felt well or were in good voice. The Lafayette Theatre on Seventh Avenue in New York was a black theatre, and there was an elm tree standing in front of it. Nobody knows why or when or how it started, but a distinct aura of good luck gathered round this tree and actors on their way to the theatre for an audition or opening would kiss it for good luck. Over the years the tree became a meeting place for actors, and when a little café was built next to it, the elm tree was put on the Broadway map. Producers and directors and agents looking for talent would go down to the elm tree and pick their fancy. It gradually became necessary to kiss it in moments of crisis, and leaves and twigs from the tree became a favorite lucky mascot. Then in 1934 it was cut down for a redevelopment, but at the request of all the black actors, the stump was left whose magic properties were considered to be no less potent than the whole tree. But it did not survive long, for shortly afterward a car ran into the stump and uprooted it and that was the sad end of the elm tree. A few months later the demolition squads moved in and that was also the end of the Lafayette Theatre.

Certain pantomimes in England are unlucky, *Robin Hood* and *Babes in the Wood* and *Aladdin*, particularly *Aladdin* because the excessive use of trapdoors and smoke and magical production effects represent a real hazard to life and limb. But *Cinderella* is a lucky pantomime and this happily overflows into any play which has a Cinderella theme. Any play in which the heroine or hero appears in rags in Act One and in beautiful clothes in Act Three, and in addition goes to a ball or party or whatever, can be truthfully described as a modern-style Cinderella. The obvious example of this is *Pygmalion*, which is nothing more than Cinderella brought up to date, and this is one reason (there are others) why *Pygmalion* is the luckiest play of this century. It is always a huge success; it always makes money. There hasn't been a day since its premiere in 1914 when it hasn't been performed somewhere in the world, and in its gold-filled history it has always made reputations. The sensational first production placed it firmly on the theatre map, the film version in 1938 brought the film industry into the international market and made a star out of Wendy Hiller and a much acclaimed director out of Anthony Asquith, and the unique epoch-making success of *My Fair Lady* needs no further comment or explanation. It's always been a very lucky play for me because the only play which ever made me any real money, and in which I was able to appear on Broadway and tour the United States was my own *The First Night of Pygmalion*.

Actors who appear regularly in pantomime and variety have their own special superstitions which are not observed or even known in what is still called the legitimate theatre. There are two popular songs that have bad-luck associations and should never be sung or hummed or whistled anywhere backstage or on stage even if the play requires it. The first is Tosti's "Good-bye," which has strong associations with death and which no singer will tolerate: Ellen Terry, though, had no such qualms, for when Tosti himself met her, he inscribed the fatal words on the back of a photograph of himself and gave it to her . . . "Goodbye, summer, goodbye" . . . She was enchanted.

The second forbidden song is from Balfe's opera *The Bohemian Girl* which contains the ever-green and ever-popular aria, "I dreamt I dwelt in marble halls." Harold Wilkinson once told me that in the twenties he had nearly been dismissed from the com-

the Arts Theatre Club. In those golden days the theatre itself was in the devoted and inspired hands of Alec Clunes, whose policy was to produce a different play every month with the best possible people. He was a fanatical admirer of Bernard Shaw and some of the finest Shavian revivals of the postwar years were at the Arts. The standard was very high even if the salaries were low. Transfers were not uncommon and many careers blossomed there. It was a period of great theatrical vitality, and the unemployed actors, nursing their sixpenny coffees and glancing irritably through *The Stage,* noticed that Alec Clunes himself, his directors, administrative staff, and the resident company would use the snack bar during their tea breaks and lunch hours. It was naturally hoped and assumed that he would use them, and a certain amount of discreet jostling, lobbying, and eye-catching did take place. Useless. It seemed that Clunes, whose apprenticeship in the theatre had not been difficult, had little sympathy for unemployed actors and was, furthermore, greatly irritated by the amount of space we took up in the snack bar and the noise we made in the course of the day (we were, admittedly, rather loud and convivial). He couldn't get rid of us, as we did represent a source of valuable income to the club, but he could refuse to employ us. He decided that nobody who was seen at all frequently in the snack bar should ever be employed in the theatre and communicated this decision privately to his staff. Nothing was ever said to us and the matter was supposed to be a dark secret, but inevitably the word did get round that the black mark was on us. It gradually became unlucky to be seen there, and thus another superstition was born. But most of us—and this group included Barry Foster, Kenneth Haigh, Robin May, Walter Hall, and Harold Pinter—continued to use it, partly because there was nowhere else to go except the Lyons Tea Shop next door which none of us liked, and partly because we just couldn't believe that the charming Alec Clunes, whom we all greatly admired as a superb actor, could be so unreasonable and so unkind. But it seemed that he could and was, and throughout the years of his management none of us ever worked there.

It's bad luck to have worked in the first productions of some-body now famous and successful. Once they have achieved this enviable state, they have a tiresome habit of consigning to outer darkness all memories of their early years and everybody as-sociated with them. To have appeared in Mr. H.'s production of *Worm's Eye View* at Manchester or Mr. G.'s production of *Life with Father* at Cape Cod twenty years ago is a fair guarantee that you will never work with either again, even if you got on well with them and were good in the part. There are, naturally, some honorable exceptions, well-balanced, secure people who don't hold it against an actor if he knew them in their dog days, but by and large this superstition appears to be justified. In fact the an-ticipation of a cold reception will serve as an active discour-agement to an actor who will not even make a preliminary ap-proach to a director or producer if he had worked with him years ago. This law applied to producers, casting directors, managers who had once been actors, to anybody who has crossed to the other side of the desk. It doesn't apply to star actors who are touchingly loyal to their colleagues of their salad days. Sir Henry Irving was well known in the profession for giving preferential treatment to the old actors he had once known in his purgatorial early years and who formed the nucleus of his Lyceum Com-pany. And many of the names in the programs of Laurence Olivier's early appearances in the twenties appeared with reassur-ing frequency in those of the forties, fifties and sixties.

The rehearsal period is when an actor is at his most supersti-tious, for then he is nervous and vulnerable. In America, nobody will blame him, for the truly appalling practice still survives whereby an actor is strictly on probation for the first five days and can be dismissed any time if the producer decides he is either mis-cast or just not good enough. The wretched actor may need the job desperately, but he has only five days to make an impression. Instead of allowing the performance to develop slowly and care-fully over the weeks, he is forced to get easy, striking effects over-

Sir Henry Irving as Shylock

night and to produce a tiresome form of instant acting which can seriously damage the final performance, just as Mr. Crummles stunted his infant daughter's growth by feeding her on gin. After five days, if the producer is satisfied, the actor will receive the protection of a contract and he can breathe again, but by then the damage may have been done. These actors sometimes try to make an impression by learning the part in advance and arriving at the first rehearsal word perfect. This is invariably a waste of time and energy because there are always cuts in the text, and an actor who has learned a section of the text which is later cut finds it very difficult to forget it. This is one reason why older actors, particularly in England, regard it as bad luck to learn the part before rehearsals start. This also may explain the strange hostility to the youthful Noel Coward of the older actors in the companies he first appeared with. Coward always knew every word of his part at the first rehearsal, and his efficiency in this matter was a source of great irritation to the others. This continued all his life, and in later years when he directed plays, particularly his own, he insisted on the company being word perfect from the start, on the grounds that you couldn't act or develop with a script in your hands. Some of the older actors in these companies just could not cope; rehearsals were particularly frustrating for them and their performances did finally suffer from those terrifying lapses of memory which we all fear. Every actor has his own method and his own pace for working and to interfere arbitrarily with this is to ask for trouble.

It's bad luck to want something too much. If an actor is bursting to play a particular classic part and has been hoping and dreaming about it all his life, and then gets his big chance, this, as the old-timers keep saying, is very unlucky. Some of the saddest theatrical disasters have stemmed from this situation and Charles Laughton's Lear—tragic in a sense Shakespeare didn't intend—is a case in point. Laughton was a frustrated classical actor. Shakespeare was his greatest love and joy and the volume of the complete works, a school prize when he was a boy, was thumbed and tattered by a lifetime of study. He dreamed of playing all the great heroic parts, but it was only after his stupendous success in the film *Henry VIII* in 1933 that Lilian Baylis invited him to the Old Vic for a season. In quick succession he played a disastrous Macbeth, a competent Henry VIII, a dullish Prospero, and an interesting Angelo, but he had not been a success, and it was quite evident that he just couldn't do Shakespeare. It was, and still is, difficult to explain why this should have been so. He was one of the most gifted and exciting actors of his day, with a strong star personality, an actor whom it was always tremendously stimulating to watch, but he had made a late entry into the profession at the age of twenty-six, and his meteoric rise to fame came after only six years and ten plays, all but two in the West End. It is tempting to think that if he had enjoyed a longer apprenticeship involving a lot more stage experience (he never acted in a repertory company; he started in London and never went out of it during those early years), he would have acquired a stronger technique and a better voice without which classical acting is impossible. He was painfully aware of this and would sometimes describe himself as a gifted amateur, one of those sad half-truths which are the hallmark of the insecure actor.

His supreme ambition was to play King Lear. In preparation for the great day when it arrived, he learned the part, planned how he would play it, rehearsed it privately in solitude, dreamed about it, thought about it, and talked about it. It rapidly became an obsession. One day, he would stride onto the stage to the shriek of trumpets and say, "Attend the Lords of France and Albany, Gloucester . . . meanwhile we shall express our darker purpose . . ." And then in 1959 he was invited to play it at Stratford on Avon. The omens were good: the sensible and sympathetic director was Glen Byham Shaw, and the company included Vanessa Redgrave, Albert Finney, Ian Holm, and Robert Hardy. On the first day's rehearsal, he asked permission to rehearse without the script. He'd known every word for thirty

Charles Laughton as Rembrandt

years and it would help him if he could just let the magical words flow. Permission being granted, he then proceeded to treat the company not to a low-keyed, cautious, first-rehearsal walk-through, but to a complete and superbly considered performance; it was powerful, passionate, and deeply moving, a tour-de-force. "This is going to be the greatest Lear we shall ever see," said the company in wonder when they finished that day's rehearsal. And so it would have been if the critics had seen it there and then. But there were six long weeks of rehearsals, and having struck his bull's-eye, Laughton couldn't keep it up. When you're at the top, the only progression is down, and so it was. Day after day he was forced to go through the performance, and it became dull and stale by repetition. Boredom and frustration set in, and as the first night approached, sheer terror took over.

This sad story had its climax on the first night which has been described by different members of that company. The first-night audience was packed and studded with celebrities, all eager and curious to make odious comparisons. Fanfare of trumpets, the stage fills up with the Court, more trumpets and on sweeps Laughton looking magnificent. He climbs up to the throne, turns round, opens his mouth to say his first line—and can't. He has forgotten it. His mind is a total blank. He is paralyzed with fear. Three actors standing nearby generously prompt him, but the gesture is useless, for he cannot hear what they say; their voices make up an indistinct trio of sound. The play has ground to a halt. Suddenly, with admirable presence of mind he points to the prompt corner. "Yes, dear?" he says, and the prompter's voice rings out loud and clear for all to hear. "Attend the Lords . . ." "Thank you," he interrupts, and having remembered the line the play can now continue. The play proceeds without further incident and Laughton manages to get through it, but the evening has had a knife-edge tension and the performance has suffered immeasurably. It was a colossal disappointment to the critics, the public, the company, and to Laughton himself. In later performances things did, of course, improve, but history, most cruelly and unjustly, is made on first nights. Laughton never really got over his disappointment. He had wanted to play Lear too much and for too long, and therein lies bad luck.

It's interesting that the same situation crops up in a famous prewar French film about an old actors' home, *Le Fin du Jour*, in which Michel Simon plays an old actor who gets his big chance. This actor had understudied Sacha Guitry for over a thousand performances at the Comedie Française in *L'Aiglon* but had never had a chance to play the part and he is bursting to do so. A life-long obsession. Now, at seventy, he is brooding resentfully over the past. Then the Comedie Française arranges a special charity matinee at the actors' home of this same play, but the leading man is taken ill and the company doesn't carry an understudy. What's to be done? The old actor volunteers eagerly, is pushed into the costume and makeup, and bundled on stage in front of a packed audience. And what happens? He can't remember a word. The other actors try to prompt him. Useless. Then he breaks down, crying through his makeup and muttering, "I knew every word of it once. . . . I'm too old now . . . every word . . . !" (Michel Simon's acting in this poignant scene was really heartbreaking.) He then has a heart attack and dies. The perpetual understudy who never played the part.

Some producers consider that first-night parties are bad luck—noisy, horribly expensive, and not much fun because the tension, while the fate of the play is being debated by the critics, plays merry hell with people's nerves and tempers. Many people consider it very bad luck to wait up for the notices in Sardi's (in New York) or at the Caprice (in London) and to then have them read out loud to the company, backers, and friends. If this is done in the complacent expectation of their being very good and they turn out otherwise, it can be just a little embarrassing. Most actors can claim some memorable experience of this.

It happened to me in Cape Town after I had opened in Shaw's *Getting Married* at the Hofmeyr Theatre and had given what I smugly thought was a very good, funny performance as Reggie.

The party at the Negrita Bar was attended by dozens of actors, backers, friends, and members of the local cultural administration. At 1 A.M., the Afrikaans papers arrived and were grabbed by the company. As I did not speak a single word of the language, I asked for the notice to be read aloud. Our stage manager, grinning broadly, obliged. "Richard Huggett gives a grotesquely unfunny, ridiculously caricatured performance. He should return to England as soon as possible!" The play did terrible business and I received an assassination threat from some South African patriots, doubtless due to my grotesquely unfunny acting.

Backstage superlatives are frowned on. To prophesy a great success and a long run before the notices appear is to ask for trouble. One old actor would go berserk if anybody said, "Darling, you'll be here for a year," and there is one old musical comedy actress who would never receive backstage visitors for a week until the Sunday notices had appeared. Her speedy exit immediately after the performance into a waiting taxi was one of the sights of the West End.

There was a particularly tragic example of the dangers of overconfidence in the London production of *That Championship Season* in May 1974. The company, lovingly assembled from the Broadway and touring casts, was led by Broderick Crawford, and everyone had good reason for optimism. The play had been running on Broadway for two years and had collected the triple crown of the Pulitzer Prize, the Tony, and the New York Drama Critics Award. If this wasn't enough, the cast was led by a onetime popular and still-remembered film star, they were housed in the charming and centrally placed Garrick Theatre facing Sir Henry Irving's statue at the bottom of the Charing Cross Road, and London in that sunny May was at its springtime best. They were so confident of success that they made all the mistakes; it was a classic example of tempting Providence. They brought their wives and families over at great expense and took long leases on their London flats. The opening performance was very smooth: individually and collectively they were superb, and their friends, filling the dressing rooms afterward, eagerly prophesied a long run. At the party afterward, the notices were delivered and read out. Disaster. They varied between the lukewarm and downright hostile, and the party broke up in embarrassment. The audiences were sparse, for whatever the considerable merits of the play, the English public had little interest in an Ibsenite drama about small-town jealousies and failures, set in one depressing room and written in an extreme form of American slang. The play was withdrawn after three humiliating weeks and five deeply unhappy American actors crept back to New York.

From time to time stories leak out of actors and actresses who have occult powers and can make bad luck come to people who displease them; these stories cease to be mere superstitions and fall fairly and squarely into the realms of the supernatural. There was once an actor named Peter Stephens whose fleshy, beaky-nosed, rather eunuchoid appearance and personality made him specially well suited to parts which called for the projection of anything evil or sinister. In 1947 he was touring in a production of *The Immortal Hour* by Clifford Bax. The star was an actress named Vera Lindsay who had married into the aristocracy, had retired from the theatre, and was now making a comeback. Peter Stephens took a violent dislike to her for reasons which were never made clear and got into the habit of making witty and malicious remarks at her expense.

One evening, after an unusually heated argument, he was heard to swear—half-jokingly, it was assumed—that he would deal with her. He went to his dressing room and fashioned a little effigy of her out of a stick of makeup, painted her face on it, and decked it with wisps of cloth he had taken from her dressing room. Further identification was found in her initials clearly written on the breasts of the effigy. Jean McConnell, who was the understudy, passed his open door and saw the effigy stuck with pins and sagging under the heat of the lights in a grotesque and horrible manner. Thirty minutes later she was informed by the stage manager that Vera Lindsay was feeling ill and would therefore not be able to perform that night. The next day, suffering from what the doctor tactfully described as an undefined illness, Vera Lindsay left the company permanently and Jean McConnell played her part for the remainder of the tour. Bernard Archard who was in the company remembers that Peter Stephens was fascinated by witchcraft, talked about it a lot, and clearly possessed an extensive knowledge of the subject. Nobody knew for certain whether or not he had occult powers, and when questioned he would smile mysteriously and make an evasive answer. Nobody knew whether this particular incident was or was not a joke which just happened to turn sour, or whether Peter Stephens did practice the black arts. In fact, it will never be known, for he is now dead.

An actor is the classic battleground between man's common sense and his superstitious fears; many of these are absurd and irrational and anybody outside the theatre might well be tempted to sneer. He should certainly not do so, for he does not know what an actor goes through before he gives his performance. This is something nobody knows except the actor himself and his immediate colleagues. It is fitting that the outsider should be told, since it is only with knowledge that he can achieve a sympathetic understanding. Let him be given a glimpse into a place he has never been and never will be allowed—an actor's dressing room on a first night. Let him see for himself just what an actor suffers in that vital half hour before the performance.

It's a very big first night in a big West End theatre, and there is the unhappy actor sweating unhappily away in his dressing room. Let us call him Michael Plinge (Walter's great-grandson). Michael is aged thirty-four and has been a professional actor for twelve years. He has had small parts in three mildly successful West End plays, each better than the last, and his career, augmented by a fair amount of television and some films, is at last beginning to take shape. The present production is a glossy revival of a famous eighteenth-century comedy with one Knight and one Dame in the star parts and supported by a very distinguished company. The first-night audience is even glossier than usual, and a large number of Very Important People have flown in from Australia, South Africa, Canada, and, of course, New York. There will certainly be a Broadway production, but whether the present company will go intact, or whether it will be only some, and if so which, these thorny questions are as yet unanswered, though rumors will circulate relentlessly throughout the run. Michael has a good supporting part and it's his best yet in the West End. Everything depends on tonight, he feels, and the fact that he has felt this no less emphatically on every West End first night doesn't diminish the urgency.

On Broadway, his opposite number could be called Rod Spelvin (grandnephew to the famous George). He is appearing at the Alvin Theatre in a new musical based on Watergate and called—how could it be otherwise—"*Henry, They're Bugging Me!*" This project has been lovingly cherished by Broadway's top writing team until what has been generally agreed to be the Right Moment, and they've beaten all the rival teams by a narrow margin (no less than a dozen reputable authors had the same idea). Broadway's most dynamic leading lady has been coaxed out of her retirement to play Martha Mitchell and by a unique stroke of showbiz genius, a singing TV cowboy star is making positively his first appearance on Broadway as Nixon. Rod Spelvin plays Kissinger, and he has one good point number in Act Two, "I'm Going Taping in the Morning. . . . Get Me to the White House on Time."

Rod is aged thirty, built on plumply fleshy lines with thinning hair and a round amiable face. Casting agents invariably put him down in their files as a Zero Mostel type, and while deeply annoyed by this handle, however accurate, he is clever enough to have turned it to his advantage. Who is a more natural choice than Rod for those parts in summer stock and on distant tours where Mr. Mostel is unlikely to appear? Rod did his two years hard labor in the Broadway production of *Fiddler on the Roof*, toured with *My Fair Lady* as Doolittle, and with *The Odd Couple* as Oscar, thus laying the foundations of his career, which began to blossom at the Cape Cod Playhouse with his starring performance in and as *The Man Who Came to Dinner*. It was this which caught the attention of a prominent and inaccessible Broadway agent who promptly arranged for him to play Zero Mostel's part in *Ulysses in Nighttown* at a dinner theatre in Washington. Here he caught the eye of Buddy Epstein who was setting up his new musical, and who noticed that Rod bore a likeness to Henry Kissinger. This train of thought resulted in a meeting, then an audition, and finally a contract.

Here he is in the tiny dressing room which he shares with an old actor-buddy, Marvin Q. Schwartz, who was with him in *Fiddler*. Rod is very pleased about this, for Marvin is fun to have around and he doesn't talk too much. Rod has been in the theatre for two hours, fully dressed and made up for the part, desperately trying to concentrate. The show has been on the road now for two months and it has been a difficult and exhausting time for everybody. Notices have varied between the lukewarm and the downright hostile, a disturbing factor in a community where nothing less than unqualified hysterical praise will persuade the paying customer to part with $20 a seat.

In common with every major production in the American musical theatre, it has been rewritten mercilessly on the tour. New numbers have been written in and then after a few days have been cut. Actors have been sacked and replaced. The second lead, playing Haldeman, walked out in Baltimore, the TV cowboy star had a nervous breakdown in Chicago, missing twelve performances, and in obedience to a long-established tradition, the English director was sacked in Boston. Four new Act One finales have been tried out and a fifth was put in only last week. The show has been reshaped, rescored, renumbered, reeverythinged almost out of recognition, the company has been rehearsing day and night, they are tired and confused, and Rod's chief anxiety at this moment is trying to remember what's cut and what's left. That witty line in Act One he's so fond of and which always got a laugh in Philadelphia, "The President is making history, but can he consume it?"—was that cut in Baltimore or not? He checks with his script, now almost illegible with the mass of black and blue pencil marks; the line was cut in Chicago, replaced in Washington, cut again in New Haven, and now replaced but instead transferred to Act Two for the Broadway opening, thus providing the lead-in for Nixon's new number "Impeachment."

Rod isn't particularly superstitious, but he does observe one curious opening-night ritual; he always goes down to a bar in Greenwich Village where an old army buddy from Vietnam works as a barman. Hank is an artist, and on these occasions does a little instant cartoon of Rod on the back of a menu card. Rod has seven of these all round the mirror. He has a pair of lucky cuff links given to him by his first wife when they met in the Actors Studio years ago and which he always wears on opening nights. All round the dressing table are photos of Dr. Kissinger; when the show was announced in *Variety*, just about everybody Rod knew sent him a picture of, and cuttings about, his distinguished original.

On Broadway, the general rule forbidding backstage visitors before a performance is not strictly enforced; indeed it hardly seems to exist. Although curtain time is at 7:30 P.M., there is no question of the play starting because the audience, furred and dinner-jacketed, is still happily screeching in the lobby. Rod now has a series of visitors, starting with his third wife, a pretty blonde, accompanied by her mother, a fleshy blonde. They present him with a sprig of white heather, kiss and hug him, and vanish. Then the press representative comes in with a man from *The New York Times* and a photographer. Rod answers politely the ineptitudes thrust at him and tells them exactly what it feels like to be impersonating Dr. Kissinger with the great man watching in the front row. Finally, with much giggling, screaming, and laughing, a girl from the chorus, called Blanche, accompanied by a party of her friends from another show, pushes her way in. She is the lucky recipient of the Gypsy Robe and Rod touches it and kisses her, relieved that the ritual is over and that he can now concentrate. At 7:26, the audience has been coaxed to its seats and the show can go on. Rod is on at the opening. He is not happy about this, not happy at all.

Back in London, Michael Plinge is sitting at his dressing table naked, except for a periwig and a pair of striped Regency shorts. All round the mirror are the telegrams and cards sent by his family, friends, and colleagues. Piled high on the table are the first-night presents he has received from the company, an unusually friendly one, he is pleased to note. There is a bottle of champagne with the compliments of the management, a silver tankard inscribed with the play's title given by the Dame, a beautiful print of Rex Whistler's famous and highly scurrilous picture of the Prince Regent in Brighton from the Knight, a box of very expensive liqueur chocolates from the director. The other presents include a wide variety of goodies to be eaten, drunk, worn, listened to, read, or just looked at. Since the sensible tradition still stands whereby you give the same present to everybody in the company, twenty-seven identical piles are standing in different dressing rooms.

The dressing room also accommodates his lucky mascots. Michael doesn't regard himself as particularly superstitious, and will deny it if asked, but the fact is that these little objects do give him a feeling of reassurance, and he would be very worried if one of them were lost. There is a 1930 penny picked up in a gutter in Brighton on the first day of his honeymoon. It is very rare and he has firmly refused all offers from fanatical numismatists. There is a tiny two-inch golliwog, given to him by his mother on his first first night in Lincoln rep. There is a medallion of St. Genesius, for he is a Catholic, and he took this with him on a pilgrimage to Rome when he was a boy and it was blessed by the Pope. There is a silver threepenny bit which was used as a prop in his first West End play, four years ago, and most important of all there is a miniature framed photo of Irving, signed in the great man's illegible handwriting. This was a present from Wingy, an old actor who befriended Michael in his first job at Lincoln and taught him much. The miniature had been given to Wingy (Wingfield C. Johnson to give him his full name and dignity) by Martin Harvey who had received it from Irving himself, so that Apostolic Succession, as Wingy used to say, was now complete.

The speaker in the dressing room suddenly comes to life. "Good evening, ladies and gentlemen, good evening. This is your half-hour call. Half an hour please. Thank you." The voice is as soothing as a stewardess's, but Walter is not soothed. He takes an eyebrow pencil and gently sketches very thin lines under his eyes to give them definition. A touch of red on the lips, a light dusting of the whole face with French chalk, and the makeup is complete.

A low rumbled muttering is heard from the end of the room. It is one of his dressing-room partners, a big, muscular, Cornishman, former boxing champion, former merchant-navy seaman who has strayed into the profession as a stunt man with a passable singing voice and has, to everybody's surprise including his own, done rather well. He is a grumbler who grumbles incessantly about every conceivable thing, and if there is nothing he will invent something. The third occupant is a pixilated little comic from Aberdeen who drenches himself in a very strong eau de cologne and twitters endlessly about his health. The fourth is a former Oxford don who has made a late entry into the profession. He would like to have directed the play, which being a classic he regards as his own special property; instead he goes around telling everybody how they should act (every company has one). In the nicest possible way, of course: "I say old boy, hope you don't mind, but you'll find it much better if you do it like this. . . ." He sports green tweeds, smokes a curved pipe, and is generally regarded as a terrible nuisance. There have been no open rows and Michael, who is a peaceful person, hopes that there won't be, but he does sometimes wonder what he has done to be landed with the three biggest bores in the company and how long he can stand it. His contract runs for a year, and if the play does like-wise, he is going to have problems.

The company manager, very smooth in an electric-blue dinner jacket and silver ruffled shirt front, puts his head round the door. "Good luck, gentlemen," he says, and out he goes. The speaker comes to life again. "Fifteen minutes, please, fifteen minutes." Twenty minutes to go. Michael now starts to put on his clothes; the white stockings, the white frilled shirt front, red satin breeches, red velvet coat, black shoes with silver buckles, lacy cravat, and three-cornered hat. He always leaves dressing till the last possible moment. This is part of the ritual, for he has read somewhere that a number of famous sporting figures do likewise, and like most actors he is a keen follower of sport.

Other members of the company come in to wish him luck, in ones and twos. Michael privately wishes that they wouldn't, for all this seems to be tempting Providence, but he allows himself to be kissed, patted, hugged, and generally stroked around. He is now bursting to pee and he goes down to the men's room, but it is a false alarm, imagination rather than nature. Back in the dressing room he hears the speaker again: "Five minutes, please, five minutes." Christ, only ten minutes to go and suddenly he realizes that he can't remember his first line. In vain he searches the corners of his memory but it won't come. In panic he grasps the script lying open on his table and hastily turns up the relevant page—yes, there it is, how could he have forgotten it? Never in four weeks of rehearsals or fifteen previews did he have any trouble. He starts mentally to go through his big speech in Act Two, but halfway through his memory falters and there is noth-ing but blankness. The whole part seems to be slipping away from him. He takes the Irving miniature and the threepenny bit and the golliwog and places them inside his pockets. Although the "beginners, please" has not yet been called, he now leaves the dressing room and walks down the echoing steps to the stage. As he walks he starts to recite his lines, remembering one of Wingy's best pieces of advice: "Run yourself in, laddie, start acting the minute you leave yer dressing room." The stage is empty and he now embarks on a complicated good-luck ritual. He walks round the empty stage, concentrating as far as possible on nothing. He touches the front curtain, he touches and kisses the wooden struts behind the scenery, and he whispers a slightly revised version of a childhood prayer of supplication, "Matthew, Mark, Luke, and John, bless the stage that I lie on." The end of this ritual is very curious. He holds out his hands in front of him and then slowly brings the two thumbs up and presses them against his forehead, concentrating on nothing but saying "not bloody likely." Wingy had passed this onto him. "Concentrates the mind most wonderfully, laddie," he used to say cheerfully, "and with a quote from *Pygmalion*, which is a very lucky play, you're off to a flying start."

Already he is feeling better but the feeling is short-lived. The stage is now filling up with the company, lounging around uneasily, exchanging whispered small talk with nervous hilarity and taking up their positions for the opening on and off the stage. And then comes the moment that every actor dreads—the raising of the safety curtain with a slow, long-drawn-out hiss. The sound of the audience which was formerly a distant rumble is now a deafening roar, the howling of animals shrieking for blood with only a thin velvet and brocade curtain between all 950 of them and twenty-eight unhappy actors.

Michael remembers with alarm that his own party is sitting in the fifth row of the stalls, consisting of his wife, his parents, an old actress friend now turned film casting director, his agent, and his agent's Jamaican boy friend. But it is not they he is worried about, for their goodwill can be taken for granted. It's the critics and other managements, the producers and directors of films and TV, in fact all those boss figures on whose collective goodwill his future depends. "Places, please," says the company manager from the prompt corner. Michael retreats to the darkness of the wings. His teeth are chattering, his legs shaking, his heart pounding so loudly that surely everybody in the theatre can hear it. He is sweating all over as though he had malaria; he feels sick, he is

sword was placed above his writing desk, the better to cast its benevolent influence, and though temptingly large sums of money
were offered to him, Gilbert never parted with it. One night,
thieves broke in and stole it, and not all Gilbert's money, influence, nor the combined efforts of the police could recover it.
From then on his fortunes declined. His next opera was *The Grand
Duke*, which was a total failure, and this was the last he and
Sullivan wrote together, for four years after that Sullivan died,
and their unique partnership was at an end.

Sullivan's lucky mascot was a handsome, middle-aged American lady, Mrs. Ronalds. She was his friend, his confidante, his
constant companion, and she brought him good luck. She was
with him in his Victoria Street flat when he was composing and,
since she had a fine voice, an extensive knowledge of music, and
was a composer herself of popular ballads, he came to rely on her
judgment. It is not known just how far she influenced the music
he wrote for the operas, but it was a matter of considerable comment that she influenced the performance. On first nights and
gala nights with royalty present, he conducted and she always sat
in the stage box where he could see her. When the audience was
applauding each number and screaming for encores, it was her
decision. If she smiled, he would allow the encore. If she didn't,
then he wouldn't. She introduced him to another of her friends,
the Prince of Wales, and through him to that colorful group of
hell-raisers, high-livers, and fornicating extroverts known as the
Marlborough House set. Mrs. Ronalds used to sing "The Lost
Chord," the ballad by Sullivan that Victorian England had taken
to its heart. The prince carried on the royal tradition of musical
philistinism by declaring that this was the supreme musical experience of his life. Mrs. Ronalds continued to bring good luck to
Sullivan throughout his life. Posterity must be grateful to her.

There were some curious first-night rituals. Caruso, being very
religious, would say the whole Rosary in the privacy of his dressing room. Luigi Ravelli, a rival tenor of note, would sing to his
dog and await his verdict. If the dog growled approvingly and

mezuzah and insisted on returning to the hotel to collect it. As a result he missed his plane, but the plane crashed over the Rocky Mountains and everybody was killed.

Animals figure prominently among singers' lucky mascots. Tito Brignoli, a tenor who was very active in America during the nineteenth century, kept a stuffed deer head. Not only did he invariably take it to the opera house, he further insisted that it be placed on the stage, and it was the stage manager's task to find a suitable place for it. It was noticed by startled operagoers that the Café Momus, the square in Seville, the countess's drawing room, even Florestan's prison cell, were all dominated by a very large deer's head which cast a stern, unsmiling stare on the scene. Over the years audiences and singers and staff became very attached to it, so when he died, the deer's head remained until it was destroyed by fire, much mourned by everybody.

Offenbach had a very curious mascot: it was a conductor's baton which had been fashioned out of a croupier's rake given to him at the casino in Baden-Baden where he had once enjoyed a very lucky evening and had won a vast sum of money. Thereafter the baton lay on his desk and piano when he was composing, and it was with this that he conducted his operas. The sensational success he enjoyed with his best known operettas after he had acquired his lucky baton was always attributed to this.

W. S. Gilbert would never have regarded himself as a superstitious man—from a soldier who embodied the nineteenth-century view of logical, rational man, such a thing would be a deplorable admission of weakness—but he did attach a certain occult power to the Japanese ceremonial sword which hung above the fireplace in his Kensington house. Savoyards all know the famous and well-documented story of how it fell with a clatter into the fireplace on a windy day and thus triggered off the chain of creative thought which led to *The Mikado*. This was the greatest success he and Sullivan were to enjoy, and the decade that followed and that produced *Ruddigore*, *The Yeomen of the Guard*, *Utopia Limited*, and *The Gondoliers* were golden years indeed. The ceremonial round the world confining their activities to the six international opera houses that really count, their repertoire limited to the dozen or so operas that suit them. As they grow older their repertoire shrinks until retirement and teaching loom up glacially before them. Operatic singers are exceedingly vulnerable to the ills of the flesh. The voice, that infinitely precious instrument, must be cuddled and coddled and cherished and cosied lest the slightest chill or breath of ill wind should spoil it and compel them to miss the performance. Walking on such a delicate tightrope of health, and with a life so limited and so dangerous, it is surprising that they are not more superstitious than they are.

There are fewer general superstitions in the opera world because, I suspect, that singers are always too busy and too ubiquitous to have time to brood, but most singers have a lucky mascot or talisman or amulet, and even a brief survey of operatic history will produce some intriguing items. Elizabeth Soederstrom travels a whole menagerie of glass animals with her, very expensive, very fragile, which must be placed in exactly the same position on her dressing-room table, and God help any dresser or intruder who breaks one. Caruso carried a number of little charms strung together on a golden ring in the pocket of his costume, and he would go mad if anybody wished him good luck. Seeing that the charms were placed in the pocket of his costume was his valet's most important duty, and the only occasion on which Caruso's patience and good temper broke down was when this was forgotten. Tebaldi set up dozens of dolls and little teddy bears on her dressing-room table and Luciano Pavarotti always picks up bent nails and keeps them, for the V sign is traditionally as good luck in opera as it was for the war effort. Melchior had a mezuzah in a gold case embellished with the Star of David picked out in diamonds and rubies. Melchior had a very deep attachment to it, not because he was Jewish, but because it once saved his life. He had left his hotel in western Canada to drive to the airport to catch a plane for New York where he was due to sing. On the way he discovered that he had forgotten to pack his precious wagged his tail, he would go happily to the opera house. If he didn't, then Ravelli would go but not happily, and his performance suffered. Jean de Reszke would place on the floor of his dressing room a tiger skin given to him by Sarah Bernhardt and would pace up and down on it, singing his part softly to himself. Kirsten Flagstad put her trust in Yoga exercises which did, it must be admitted, keep her body and voice in astonishingly good shape throughout her long and glorious career. Carl Ebert, who produced the Glyndebourne operas before the war, would rap the stage floor with his knuckles, whereas Wagner went further; he would kneel down and kiss it.

Swedes have one very peculiar superstition which is not observed by singers of any other nationality. Before they go onto the stage, they regard it as exceedingly good luck to be kicked on the bottom. It has been suggested that the reason for this odd form of masochism is that it is a willing sacrifice to the gods to ensure their goodwill. Melchior invariably suffered this mild indignity from his wife.

There is a hilarious account of the Swedish mezzo, Gertrude Wittergen, making her debut at the Met in the late thirties. On her first night there in *Aida*, her Swedish dresser, who would have executed the kick, was ill, and Wittergen was reluctant to go on the stage until this little ritual had been performed. As she spoke no English and the stage staff no Swedish, she had a problem. She was obliged to indicate her requirements in mime, a language which is traditionally open to misunderstanding. It seemed from contemporary accounts that her attempt to explain to a couple of uncouth, gum-chewing stagehands just what she wanted them to do to Amneris right there and then in the darkness of the wings caused some confusion. It was a scene worthy of the Marx brothers, and since a scene not unlike this did occur in that classic, *A Night at the Opera*, it is tempting to suspect that the author did hear about it. It seems that the message did penetrate, the kick was administered in the right place, albeit with a trifle more enthusiasm and vigor than she had expected, and a slightly bruised and breathless Amneris finally took her place in the Temple of Ra.

Melba, though in every respect a tough, hardheaded, unsentimental Australian, did have two lasting superstitions: she thought it was very good luck to be paid in cash before a performance, having once been left stranded by an unscrupulous management with a worthless check. From then on she would not take one step onto the stage until her five hundred golden guineas had been counted out in her presence, locked in a trunk, her maid installed on top of it, and the dressing room locked and bolted until after the performance. The other one was a belief that seminal fluid was not only health-giving and life-enhancing but particularly good for the vocal chords and kept them fresh and young. It is believed that she dosed herself throughout her career on performance nights. There was, apparently, no shortage of willing donors—stagehands, hotel bellboys, and colleagues in the company. No firsthand confirmation of this is forthcoming, but, if it is true, then the ritual was certainly very effective, for she continued to sing right till the end of her long life. Even at seventy her voice retained a quality which the critics, by a strange ironic twist, would always describe as fresh, pure, and virginal.

The evil eye is an ancient Italian superstition. This is what witches and people in league with the forces of evil are supposed to possess and with which they can bring about bad luck to their victims. Every Italian singer in history has gone in mortal fear of it and their memories are full of references to it. Offenbach was supposed to have it, though this may well have been circulated by his anti-Jewish rivals in the French opera and in any case didn't stop managements from accepting his operas and players from performing under his direction. Patti once conceived a violent hatred for Madame Gerster, a Hungarian mezzo with whom she once sang in *Norma*. She believed that Gerster had the evil eye, and every hitch, every piece of trouble, was laid at her door. When they took their curtain calls together, and Gerster was

Melba—of the fresh, pure, and virginal voice

cheered more loudly than Patti, she exploded with wrath and slapped her rival's face. The audience turned very nasty and booed the temperamental Queen of Song who thereafter refused to have anything to do with Madame Gerster.

Clara Kellogg, an American soprano who enjoyed considerable success at Covent Garden in the 1860s, wrote with great bitterness about her traumatic debut there in *La Traviata*. Everything went wrong from torn costumes, missing jewelry, spilled face powder to falling scenery. Small, irritating little bad-luck things happened to everybody in the company, and from time to time as the evening limped on, she noticed the company making the traditional sign that wards off the effects of the evil eye. After the performance the mystery was solved. It was the Russian-born mother of the popular actor, Richard Mansfield, who was sitting in the stage box. Her eyes were large and dark and baleful, and her personality was formidable, but whether the eyes were evil or not was never discovered.

Italian singers are more prone than any other nationality to attributing bad luck to the presence of a single evil person, known as a *iettaturo*. This jinx-laden performer can be a chorister, a principal, a member of the audience, or somebody on the stage staff. Beniamino Gigli invariably carried little sacks of garlic, fatal for social life but wonderful for salads and for repelling the powers of evil. He would distribute these little bags round his person, his house, and his dressing room, his costume, and would even try to persuade others to carry them also. A famous Russian singer placed his faith in little bags of human excrement which he believed would frighten off evil spirits. They did, but they also frightened off everybody else as well. But there is a magic talisman that effectively cancels out the effect of the evil eye, and it is a complex device consisting of a hand, a horn, and a hunchback. A popular good-luck card in Italian opera circles will show these three. Any deformity is attributed to diabolical influence, and Tettrazini would never sing if by chance she met on her way to the opera house either a one-legged man, a cross-eyed person, or a hunchback. Since most opera companies employ at least one hunchback to give color to the chorus and crowd scenes, he would be told to keep well out of the way on the nights the great singer was around. However, most singers believe a hunchback brings good luck and to be kissed by one brings even better, which perhaps explains the extreme popularity of *Rigoletto*. There is an impressive list of unlucky operas, of which *Tristan und Isolde* is perhaps the earliest. Wagner was very superstitious about it, his own special favorite from his middle period. In the century since it was first performed it has had a strange jinx on it. There were many difficulties in getting it produced at all, and, although it did go into rehearsal in Vienna in 1859 for performance at the Stadtopera, it was abandoned by the company as being unsingable and unstageable. This verdict seems inconceivable now, but it did then represent a powerful body of influential musical opinion of the time. It was partly due to the inadequacy of the tenor who was due to sing Tristan and partly due to the failure of the conductor to give an even adequate account of the exceedingly complex score, a score which had been composed during a very nerve-racking period of domestic strife, of debt, financial worries, and self-doubt. It was six years before a presentation could be arranged, in Munich in 1865 under the command and supervision of Ludwig II of Bavaria, Wagner's patron and fairy godfather. There had been endless delays, postponements, and setbacks, but on June 10 it was ready. Two disasters took place on that day.

The first was the arrival of the bailiffs to turn Wagner out of his house and seize all his furniture, the result of a lawsuit brought about by a French woman who had lent Wagner a large sum of money five years earlier. Only the prompt action of the Bavarian treasury spared him the public humiliation of being made homeless. The second was much more serious—an accident affecting Malvina Schnoor. Malvina and Ludwig Schnoor, her husband, were the original Tristan and Isolde, two singers of exceptional quality who embodied everything Wagner could possibly want for these two immensely difficult parts. On the day before the opening, Malvina took a vapor bath and promptly lost her voice. Postponement was inevitable and Wagner's many enemies were loud in their triumph. The performance finally took place three weeks later on June 10 in front of the king and six hundred guests. For the first time Bavarian music-lovers were hearing music that was really new. They did not understand it and their reception was cold. Only the king understood and loved it and commanded two more performances. They were destined to be the last for a long time, because two days after the third, Ludwig Schnoor died. His last words were "Farewell, Siegfried," a part he had been promised and which he would definitely have sung if he had lived. He was the first Tristan and possibly the greatest. It was years before Wagner could bring himself to conduct the opera or even permit its performance.

Ludwig II was abnormally shy, very neurotic, and superstitious about a number of different things. He disliked people and considered it bad luck to be too close to them, hence the fairy-tale castles which he constructed where he could live alone in total solitude. This had a predictable effect on his theatregoing. When Wagner composed *Die Meistersinger von Nürnberg* and announced it for production, Ludwig insisted on having the first performance for himself alone. Nobody else was to be allowed inside the theatre lest their coughs and shifting might distract him. *Meistersinger* was a huge success, not only with the king, but also with the public who were later admitted, and thereafter it became a good-luck ritual for Wagner to have the first performance given for the king alone. When the Festspielhaus opened in Bayreuth for the opening of *The Ring of the Nibelungen*, it was arranged for Ludwig to be there alone to enjoy in solitude what was in effect a preview. Richter conducted, Ludwig Betz sang Wotan, and Wagner sat with the king in the royal box. The performances were hugely successful, though there were a few trifling mishaps—the River Rhine overflowed its banks a trifle too enthusiastically, Valhalla burned down rather more than anybody had anticipated, and the dragon lost his head. This had been ordered from Nathans in London who enjoyed an international reputation as a theatrical costumer and property maker. But as Bayreuth was then unknown, a clerk in the mailing department sent it by mistake to Beirut on the coast of North Africa.*

If Ludwig's love of theatrical solitude was regarded by his court and people as a form of madness, then there was a good deal of method in it. Wagner can be best appreciated in an empty theatre with no audience to distract you as I discovered in the summer of 1965. As I had just been in *Moses and Aaron* at Covent Garden and had met some of the staff, I was given access to the dress rehearsals of the four parts of *The Ring* on four successive mornings. My seat in the grand tier overlooked an empty house, and the impressive cathedral hush added immeasurably to the impact of the music. Never did I ever hear the *Ring* again in such superb conditions.

There are a number of unlucky operas, all very popular and constantly being performed. *La Forza del Destino* was commissioned by the Russian Imperial Court and first performed in St. Petersburg but was very coldly received by an audience of hostile Russian composers and their supporters. A number of fatalities have taken place during *Forza*. Ettore Bastianini, the baritone, was taken ill with a fit of convulsions and had to retire from singing, while Pietro Cimara, a conductor, died of a heart attack while conducting a performance in Milan. It was during *Forza* that a chandelier fell into the crowded stalls, and during another performance that the theatre burned down with many fatalities. Toscanini always regarded it as his unlucky opera, and throughout his long career always refused to conduct it. It seemed that

* Lest anybody be tempted to sneer at the ignorance of the Victorians, it must be firmly stated that exactly the same mistake was made by an employee of Decca Recording Company in 1951. He received an urgent request for a box of recording tapes from the engineers in Bayreuth and sent them to Beirut. The recording was not made because the tapes did not arrive in time. The opera in question was *Tristan und Isolde*.

when he had played the cello in the Rome Opera House orchestra, a number of small accidents had happened during *Forza*. He broke a string, he was knocked over by a cab while on his way to a rehearsal, and to cap it all, one of his colleagues in the orchestra suddenly went mad, rushed home, and killed his wife with a bread knife.

The most widely publicized of all the *Forza* disasters was the tragic death of Leonard Warren on March 4, 1960, while in the middle of "*Solenne in quest' ora.*" He collapsed on the stage and died in the wings while the understudy was rushed on and the opera continued. It was Hollywood's favorite backstage cliché brought to life. "What a way to go, the end all theatre people dream of," the newspapers said the next day. More than any other opera, *Forza* fills opera singers with superstitious fears. At the mention of the name, they cross themselves and grab whatever lucky mascots are at hand. Many refuse to perform in it and some will even refuse to see it.

Other operas on the singers' black list include *The Tales of Hoffmann* because the composer died before he finished it, *Turandot* for the same reason and because a great fire broke out at the Ring Theatre in Vienna where it was staged, causing much loss of life and damage. Puccini died at his desk while writing the final scene of *Turandot*, and the final duet was finished by his friend, the composer Franco Alfano. Also on the list is Halévy's *La Juive*. Caruso became ill during a performance of this once-popular opera and died shortly afterward. Giovanni Martinelli tried it and he, too, became ill and from then on the opera dropped out of the repertoire. John Brownlee, the Australian tenor, once missed death by inches when a chandelier dropped in front of him during a performance of *The Marriage of Figaro* and thereafter viewed the opera with caution.

In England, Gluck's *Orfeo ed Euridice* has very bad luck associations ever since Kathleen Ferrier's appearance at Covent Garden. She was in great pain throughout the second performance and died a little later, painfully, of cancer (1953). Sophie Fedorovitch, who designed that production, also died a few weeks later, and since then a number of singers of note have firmly refused to appear in it.

One of the most unlucky operas is ironically the most popular of all. It has notched up more performances in its hundred years than any other and is constantly being declared by musicologists and critics as being the perfect opera, and a unique and imperishable masterpiece. Everybody knows that the first performance of *Carmen* was a failure, and if it wasn't quite the disaster which some of the more sensational musical histories have said, there is no doubt that its lukewarm reception from public and critics was a colossal disappointment to the composer. Bizet retired to the country to calm his shattered nerves, to nurse his angina pectoris, and to study the notices which had the not unexpected effect of causing a total nervous breakdown. The plot, he learned, was incoherent and immoral, Carmen was a highly unsuitable person to be the heroine of a romantic opera (whoever heard of an opéra comique being set in a cigarette factory?). The music had no melody—a verdict that seems incomprehensible to us now—and musical opinion was divided between those who thought it was too Wagnerian and those who thought it wasn't Wagnerian enough. And since when did an opéra comique have an unhappy ending?

This was Bizet's reward for six months' inspired hard work. In fact the situation was not quite as bad as he imagined. Word of mouth was performing its usual miraculous cure. As one performance followed another, the audiences grew larger and more enthusiastic, but whether Bizet knew this in his retreat and whether he would have been reassured if he had, history does not relate. Within three months there had been twenty-three performances which, by any standards, spells success. When did a modern opera do as well in present times? But on the evening of the twenty-fourth performance, June 2, 1875, a rather curious and disturbing incident occurred in Act Three when Carmen sees her death and that of Don José in the cards. The singer was Marie-Gallie who was believed to have psychic powers. When she looked at the cards, she burst into tears, collapsed over the table, and had to be led off stage, sobbing and unable to finish. She said that she had seen very bad news in the cards, something that had nothing to do with the opera but it would have its effect on all their lives. She refused to say any more and went home, pale and silent. The following day the director of the opera, M. Camillie du Locle, received a telegram. Bizet had died very suddenly of a heart attack. Carmen had claimed her first real-life victim.

Singers have ever since had a superstitious fear of the opera, believing that on its first performance in a new production or a new opera house, something will go wrong. Fanchon Thompson, making her debut at the Met, suffered a disastrous lapse of memory and had to walk off the stage, thus bringing the opera to a complete standstill. Toni Ravelli, a famous tenor of the 1880s, suddenly went mad in Act Three and tried to kill his Carmen, the American Minnie Hauck, with a knife. He was jealous of her success and in the intermission rushed round the stage shouting, "I will kill her, I will kill her." He was eventually calmed down and the fourth act proceeded without incident. Ravelli was replaced for further performances, and he retired from the operatic stage shortly afterward.

The embarrassment which every woman once feared in the days of knickers did occur to Calvé, who was regarded as the greatest Carmen of her time, which was the nineties. She was giving a Royal Command performance at Windsor Castle in front of Queen Victoria who had a great admiration for the singer and had announced her intention of decorating her after the performance. In the middle of Act Two, Calvé lost her knickers; they fell to her feet, but with admirable presence of mind she kicked them into the wings while not missing a note. Alas, her professionalism was wasted; the old queen was deeply shocked, neither smiled nor applauded at the end, and retired without presenting the medal.

It was at the Met in 1905 that a high wooden bridge at the back of the stage collapsed in Act One, throwing dozens of choristers and extras onto the stage with bruises, cuts, contusions, and a couple of broken limbs to mark the occasion. In Padua in 1920 the Russian singer, Anita Clinowa, miscalculated the distance she had to stab her Don José with the dagger, missed and struck her other colleague, Dancairo, blinding him for life. An outdoor performance in Verona was ruined by a tornado which broke the scenery into matchwood and caused a stampede among the audience which resulted in a dozen fatalities. The latest disaster connected with the opera was the appointment of Goeran Gentele to the directorship of the Met following the long reign of Sir Rudolf Bing. Gentele planned to inaugurate his tenure with a new and exciting production of *Carmen*. Preliminary conferences were held with his production team, the principal parts were cast, the designs were approved, and Gentele left for a month's holiday in Italy before returning to start rehearsals. Six days later he was killed in a car crash. Carmen had claimed yet another real-life victim, and as the opera is irredeemably popular and nothing will stop singers from singing it, there will doubtless be plenty more.

Good-luck wishes in the operatic world are more repulsive and less hygienic than in the theatre. In Germany they spit three times, or they recite the sound which spitting is traditionally supposed to make which is *toi-toi-toi*. It is in Germany that *Hals und beinbruch* (break a leg) originated. In France they also spit and say something even more distasteful, *merde-merde-merde*. In Italy it is *in bocca di lupo* which means "in the mouth of the wolf," and the translation of what they say to each other in Russia is "to the Devil with your granddaughter." In all cases the basic principle is that these will frighten away the evil spirits, and that if you wish evil, then good will come. It's an interesting theory, and one can only devoutly hope that it is borne out by the practice.

In Germany it is bad luck to get your hair cut during the rehearsals if it is either a new opera or a new production of an old opera, another example of the Samson myth in operation. This led to an unexpected crisis at Glyndebourne when some members of the chorus recruited from Berlin and Stuttgart and Munich refused to get their hair cut when rehearsing for *The Marriage of Figaro*, and the periwigs had to be made a little larger to accommodate them. In Austria you must never walk onto the stage with your overcoat and hat on, and you must never use the backstage lift during a performance. Good sense this, though; supposing you were trapped by a power cut just before your entrance? And if you drop your score onto the ground, you must stamp your foot before you bend down to retrieve it, and some singers will never bend down for any reason. Somebody else must pick it up for them.

In setting up and preparing for an operatic performance, it is the good-luck custom to place the furniture in position first and the scenery second. This is because the furniture is very big and it would not be possible to get it onto the stage otherwise. While it is waiting, the furniture is stacked up downstage in front of the footlights, and it is considered very bad luck to sit on it. This is due to the ever-present possibility of the iron safety curtain coming down unexpectedly and with lethal effect. The curtain is very heavy, it descends with terrifying speed, and frequently without any warning other than a serpentine hiss. Ron Mullenger, who stage-managed a season of opera in Belfast, remembers a man being killed in this way and a number of other mutilations and near fatalities. In fact it was only his prompt action that saved a local stagehand from having his hand chopped off by the rapidly descending curtain.

Animal excreta have a valuable good-luck property in operatic circles. In the final week of technical dress rehearsals of *Moses and Aaron* at Covent Garden in 1965, the camel, on hire from Whipsnade Zoo, deposited his candid opinion of Schonberg on the stage. This occasioned high hilarity from the four hundred people on the stage, but also a good deal of angry mumbling from the stage staff who could not decide which of their various unions should deal with it. The rehearsal was stupidly held up while the matter was being debated. It was a very exalted member of the musical staff who finally lost his temper and grabbed a shovel. "Enough of this bloody nonsense," he shouted as he leaped onto the steeply sloping ramp of the stage, "*I* will clear it up," and he did. This whole incident was regarded by the older singers as a very lucky omen, an opinion justified by the huge success of the opera which was fully sold out for all its six performances and received notices which press officers can only dream about.

Ballet dancers work harder than anybody else in the theatre and thus have little time for introspection, neuroses, and occult fantasies. Their work schedule and the physical strain involved in keeping their bodies in peak condition and their performance up to standard would make an athlete wince. Classes all morning, rehearsals all afternoon, performances most evenings, it's a hard, grueling life from nine in the morning till well after ten at night. There is no relaxation even on those exhausting one-night-stand tours with which ballet companies augment their incomes and their reputations.

An actor or a singer can sleep all morning, and laze around all day before going to the theatre, where sometimes no more is required of them than a number of speeches or a couple of arias followed by a late-night supper with his friends. An actor's work, though frequently nerve-racking is not physically exhausting (though parts like Othello and Peer Gynt are), but a dancer's life is a very hard one. It is also a very short one, with an average of twenty years, for by the time a singer is coming into his prime, the dancer is already thinking of retirement. Ballet is a very young art. Apart from *Giselle*, which dates back to 1841, ballet as we know it started with Tchaikovsky and Petipa in Russia in the late 1880s, and for all practical purposes it started here in the West in 1910 with Diaghilev and his Russian Ballet. Seventy years is not really long enough for an art form to have acquired its own legends, traditions, and mystique, nor has it. The balletic world is astonishingly and healthily free of superstitions.

There are, however, a few intriguing items. Dancers always spit onto the ribbons of their ballet shoes before tying them, for spittle represents strength and good luck. You must never hook a tutu downward, for this is bad luck. It must always be upward, for then your career will go upward and from dancing third cygnet you will end up dancing Princess Aurora. Black safety pins are unlucky and so are lilacs which must never be included in floral tributes. More than one prima ballerina has refused a bouquet when the offending flower was seen lurking in the middle of all those roses and carnations. But the ballet *Lilac Garden* is very popular and successful provided that the flowers on the stage are not real.

It's considered good luck to prick your fingers and draw blood when you're sewing on your ballet shoes. This represents a sacrifice and literally a blood offering to the deities. Dancers preparing their shoes for performance have strange rituals: some break their stiffness by cutting the soles with a knife, some by bending them in the hinge of a door, some by taking out the inner sole, or slitting open the upper and extracting the cotton padding; but whatever is done, it's bad luck to prepare more than two shoes at a time, for this would be tempting Providence. Some dancers are regarded as lucky mascots by their colleagues, and it is not unknown for one dancer to allow only another dancer in the same dressing room to hook up her tutu. Dancers often knock the stage floor three times for luck, and it has been reported that some of the Royal Ballet dancers go down and kiss it, but the stage floor at the Royal Opera House, Covent Garden, enjoys a worldwide notoriety for its dangerously uneven surface. Dancers are superstitious about their artificial curls. The dresser must not handle them, and the dancer will herself take them back to the wardrobe for overnight storage after each performance. Hersey Pigott, a dresser at the Royal Opera House, once collected the curls from the dressing room and thus provoked a storm of anger from the wardrobe mistress. An alien hand, she was firmly told, must never, never touch them.

Diaghilev, like so many Russians, was deeply superstitious, but the belief that really haunted his life was the bad luck of the sea. He had been told by a gypsy that he would die on water, and for that reason he avoided sea voyages whenever possible, for they were torture to him. But as his seasons of ballet in London were so successful and important, he was forced to take a great many trips across the Channel. He would always go down below to the saloon and sit huddled miserably in a chair with his back to the sea, muffled in a blanket covering his beaver overcoat. Though not religious he would clutch his icon of St. Nicholas and mutter prayers in an angry whisper. After an hour of inaction he would start to rage against the English, their inedible food, their ghastly weather, their unattractive girls, the ignorant philistine public; even the language did not escape censure, which he likened to the barking of dogs and frogs. Only when he safely landed at Dover did he relax and then it was sunshine and smiles. In fact, he didn't die by drowning as he had feared, but the gypsy's prophecy did come true. He died in Venice in 1929, which by extension can be described as being on water. He is buried there.

Pavlova was regarded by her superstitious company (mostly English charmingly disguised with Russian names) as being a source of good luck. For years of touring, nothing ever went wrong: no earthquakes, storms, or revolutions ever happened when the Pavlova Company was circulating round the world. They never had a rough Channel crossing in spite of adverse weather forecasts. They believed that she was under some mysterious sort of divine protection, and with her shrewd awareness of public relations and company morale, she encouraged this belief. The nearest they ever came to disaster was in America when the train carrying them had to cross a very shaky bridge and it did finally collapse but only after they had safely crossed to the other side.

Pavlova was superstitious about strangers in the wings, regarding them as harbingers of bad luck. If she saw one, however dis-

Her company believed Pavlova was under divine protection.

tinguished or in whatever authoritative company, she would walk off the stage and refuse to continue till he or she had left the theatre. She was superstitious about curtain presents. She would not allow anything but flowers to be handed up at the end of the performance. On one occasion a statue of the Madonna and Child was brought onto the stage and presented to her. When the curtain finally descended, she ran to her dressing room, weeping loudly, which was regarded by the apprehensive company as a very bad omen. Once in Berlin she was presented to the Kaiser after a performance. As she bent down to kiss his white glove, she left there a trace of scarlet lipstick. The Kaiser made a joke about it, saying that he now had blood on his hands, but Pavlova was deeply distressed by the incident. Shortly afterward, World War I started and nothing would convince Pavlova that the lipstick was not a bad omen, and that she herself was in some way responsible for the carnage that followed. The date of that sinister little incident, as she realized with alarm, was October 13, 1913. Her final performance in England at the Golders Green Hippodrome was marked by a big laurel wreath. She took it home and stayed up all night with it, surrounded by candles. She forgot to say good-bye to her swans in her London home, Ivy House, and two months later, in January 1931, she died in Amsterdam.

All her life she had been superstitious about a short ballet that had been arranged for her, *Danse Macabre*, from the Saint-Saëns music. After its first performance, which was enthusiastically received, she declared that she felt frightened and nervous, and in spite of incessant public request, she never danced it again nor allowed any of her company to do so. Naturally, its association with death would be alarming. The only other ballet that has distinct bad-luck associations is the *Rite of Spring*. It had its world premiere at the Théâtre des Champs Élysées in 1913, clearly an unlucky year for the ballet. Stravinsky's music was horribly new to the conservative ears of the Parisien public, and Nijinsky's choreography was incomplete and, in the eyes of many, totally obscene. The performance was one of the best-documented theatrical disasters of the century, when the audience started to hiss and boo and shout and scream from the beginning, with fights and face-slappings breaking out all over the house, the police were called in to eject the hooligans, Stravinsky rushed in panic backstage to find Nijinsky screaming abuse at the dancers from the wings and Diaghilev in tears all over the Champs Élysées. There seems to have been a slight jinx on the ballet. There have been very few attempts to revive it. Its complex rhythms and atonal dissonances are still a formidable stumbling block to all but a few very daring choreographers, and the few that have been mounted have not been successful, with the possible exception of Kenneth MacMillan's for the Royal Ballet.

Nijinsky was superstitiously attached to the ballet *Le Spectre de la Rose* and was very hostile to any suggestions that anybody else should dance it. Even if he had no actual control over the copyright—which was Fokine's—the ballet had been created for him and was always associated with him. It had been one of his greatest successes and to let lesser feet touch it was to court disaster. Happily, no lesser feet did touch it in his lifetime, and revivals of it since his death have shown how dependent it is on its creator. His costume covered with rose petals was a lucky mascot, and although he was offered a fortune in cash by his admirers for just one rose petal as a souvenir, he always refused. To have parted with just one would have been bad luck. Nijinsky liked money just as much as anybody else, but his rose petals were sacred. In fact, they were gradually sold off, and the culprit, who did it without Nijinsky's knowledge, was Vassiliev, Diaghilev's bodyguard.

The cinema is shorter-lived than the ballet, for all practical purposes no more than sixty glorious years, but since the actors and actresses were for the most part recruits from the theatre bringing with them their own traditions and since the industry had flowered and matured in the enclosed, hothouse world of Hollywood, the cinema is not without superstitions.

dated from the day she let it grow, another example of the Samson myth; it was down to her waist before she consented to have it trimmed to reasonable length. Godfrey Cambridge never bends down to retrieve dropped money or a bar of soap if he happens to be in the shower. Spencer Tracy never returned to collect a forgotten object, for this was bad luck, while Jeanette Macdonald, when braiding her hair, always started with her left hand; in addition she would never bend down to button up her shoes, she would always bring up the shoe to a chair. Dorothy Lamour considered it bad luck to drop an umbrella and pick it up herself; it had to be picked up by somebody else, and if there was no one near, she would leave it. Tyrone Power thought it bad luck to eat baked potatoes on a Friday. Lionel Barrymore had a dread of Rubinstein's Melody in F, which a violinist friend of his had once played immediately before his death by heart attack. Boris Karloff's great success had been the monster in *Frankenstein*. From then on he always used the same dressing room, walked down the same corridor to get to it, and always entered the studio by the same gate. He insisted on the same dresser, the same makeup man, and the same table in the studio cafeteria.

Certain people have been lucky. For years John Wayne regarded Ward Bond as lucky and made sure that he was in all his pictures, until Bond achieved independent fame in an immensely popular TV series. David Niven had similar feelings about his old wartime friend, Michael Trubshawe, and likewise employed him in a number of his postwar films. Elinor Glyn, the English novelist, and author of *It* and *Three Weeks*, made herself a very powerful force in Hollywood. With her striking, red-haired beauty, her distinguished bearing and aristocratic manner, she had no trouble in convincing the tycoons that she was a person of immense importance. Louis B. Mayer was convinced that she possessed occult powers and refused ever to make a decision without consulting her. Should this actress be put under contract? Should this actor play this part? Should this property be bought for filming? Madame Glyn was sent for and her advice urgently requested. It seemed that her influence was considerable, and many careers either blossomed or were nipped in the bud following a discreet word from Madame Glyn. She claimed that she received her occult powers from a vase which was supposed to talk to her and tell her what to do.

Alfred Hitchcock has a very unusual and striking lucky mascot—himself. He has long been of the opinion that he will bring good luck to his films if he is in them, however briefly, and the idea seems to be justified. His films are enormously successful and have long since been accepted as classics. The magic words "Alfred Hitchcock Presents" are a guarantee not only of superbly polished film-making but also of first-class entertainment. He is the only director who invariably gets star billing above the title, who is more important than any stars he cares to employ, and who can successfully make films without them. As long as anybody can remember, he has been making tiny personal appearances in his films, and these are eagerly awaited by his admirers and the subject of delighted speculation and discussion—walking across a traffic-filled road (*Psycho*), walking down a pavement (*Rear Window*), carrying a double-bass case as he gets off a bus (*Strangers on a Train*), a face in a newspaper advertisement (*Lifeboat*), a neon-lit sign outside a skyscraper (*Rope*).

In its short lifetime, the cinema has managed to produce not so much an unlucky film as an unlucky story. Cleopatra has exerted a powerful fascination over the imaginations of producers, scriptwriters, and actresses. Many films about her have been produced, some based on existing stage plays, some original film scripts, but all but one have been disastrous. The pattern is predictably the same: Mr. Z, a producer, decides that a multimillion-dollar spectacular will solve his and his studio's problems and Miss X sees herself in the part. The film is budgeted to money beyond the dreams of Cecil B. De Mille, dozens of superstars and ministars are signed up, some to speak only a single line. The publicity drums scream and shriek out their glad tidings. The producer exceeds his budget by untold millions, and in spite of the impressive display of talent in every department, the result is a dull mess with only a few oases of interest in the desert of boredom. De Mille's *Cleopatra* (1935) was laughed off the screen at its last showing at the Starlight Film Club, which isn't surprising in view of such gems of Hollywood history dialogue as, "Poor Calpurnia, the wife is always the last to know!" delivered with barely concealed mirth by Claudette Colbert. When Gabriel Pascal produced his film of Shaw's very uncinematic play *Caesar and Cleopatra* in 1944, he successfully bankrupted the British Film Industry and killed all chances of other Shaw plays being filmed for many years (*The Doctor's Dilemma* was the next, some fifteen years later). It resulted in great tensions and clashes between those involved, some of whom never spoke to each other again, and although the acting from a cast which was the cream of English talent was individually superb, the film was very badly directed—by Pascal himself, which everybody agreed was a mistake—and it amounted to two and a half hours of unadulterated tedium. For Vivien Leigh there was tragedy as well as boredom. While she shivered on the location desert at Denham studios, she miscarried and lost the baby she and Laurence Olivier were expecting. Though she was not superstitious, it seemed clear that there was a curse on the subject.

There is no reason to give a blow-by-blow account of the Burton/Taylor *Cleopatra* except to say that more than one newspaper show-biz columnist headed his article "The Curse of Cleopatra." The start in England with Peter Finch and Stephen Boyd, the cancellation of the film due to bad weather, the transfer to Rome, the happy substitute of Burton and Rex Harrison, the endless delays, the difficulty of finding a suitable script (Mankiewicz was reduced to writing each evening the scenes he was to shoot the next day; throughout the film he seldom remained more than one day ahead), and finally the cost that soared up to $37 million and elicited the most savage notices of the decade from critics who were waiting eagerly for the kill.

Happily, this did not deter Charlton Heston from directing

and starring in a long-cherished project to film Shakespeare's highly cinematic play. With a hand-picked supporting cast and all the right locations, he produced a film that was totally faithful to Shakespeare, received respectful notices, played to empty houses in London, and failed to find a distributor in America.

There are other unlucky film subjects. Lawrence of Arabia was a figure who fascinated film producers during and after his lifetime, and it was Alexander Korda who first set up a film of *The Seven Pillars of Wisdom* in 1935 to star Walter Hudd, an up-and-coming young actor who had played a part very like Lawrence in Shaw's *Too True to be Good*. The publicity and excitement were enormous, and Lawrence promised his full cooperation. Korda took his actors and film unit to the Jordan desert and some marvelous footage was shot. Suddenly Lawrence was killed in a motorcycle accident, and for reasons that have never been properly explained, the film was abandoned. It was a shocking disappointment for everybody, particularly Walter Hudd, who saw his chances of truly international stardom snatched away from him. Although he lived to do some very distinguished work in films (*Major Barbara*) and stage (the 1950 Old Vic season), he remained to his death a very difficult and embittered old man. In the postwar years, Anthony Asquith set up a new version of the story with Dirk Bogarde playing Lawrence. This too went out to the desert and was likewise abandoned under speedy and rather mysterious circumstances. In this case the jinx was eventually laid, and it was David Lean who brought good luck to Lawrence's ghost in 1960 with his superb and extremely successful *Lawrence of Arabia*, which made an overnight superstar of Peter O'Toole.

The other unlucky subject is Diaghilev/Nijinsky. There have been many attempts to set up a film of their enthralling relationship and achievements, the first being Charles Laughton and the young Anton Dolin in 1938 to be produced by Alexander Korda. Partly owing to Korda's truly Hungarian inability to make up his mind and Laughton's nervous insecurity about everything he did and the slightly restricting existence of Nijinsky himself in England, the film was abandoned. In recent years Ken Russell has tried to set up another version with Paul Scofield as Diaghilev and Rudolf Nureyev to dance and act Nijinsky, but no backing was forthcoming. In the eyes of many producers the subject is offbeat, noncommercial, and deeply suspect.

Fans are often regarded as bad luck. Not, of course, the armies of enthusiasts who besiege the stage doors and pester their divinities for autographs in the street, but fan clubs, those highly organized societies with monthly letters, mailing lists, badges, and membership branches all over the world. Fans like these are jealous, possessive, and demanding: if the star wants to change her hair style, clothing, or performances, if she wishes to play comedy instead of drama, or to do Shakespeare instead of musicals, or to marry somebody unsuitable, then the loudest opposition will come from the fan clubs. In the bad old heyday of Hollywood, fans wielded a terrifying power over their divinities, and many of the stars would not make any decision affecting their work until the fans had been consulted. Fans were avid for sensation and scandal; messy divorces, nervous breakdowns, contract-breaking, and hell-raising were all grist to their mill. They are consumed by a terrible death wish and nothing less will satisfy them. "They want me to die," said Judy Garland with a flash of alarming foresight, "they *want* me to die and they'll kill me if they can!" and obligingly she did to the crocodile tears of her fans who had encouraged her drunken tantrums, her drug-ridden unpunctuality, and all the excesses of her unprofessional behavior. Many stars have had a superstitious distaste for the whole sordid business and have refused, beyond coaxing, to have a fan club. Of course, the club can exist without the approval of the star but without some cooperation in way of an annual personal appearance at the fan-club tea party or an occasional letter for the magazine, the club will not survive for long.

There appears to be a jinx on the part of Jesus Christ, and

many actors consider it bad luck to play it; it's surprising how many actors can confirm this from their personal experience. Charles Houston, the English actor, is a case in point: in 1960 his career was shaping up nicely—leading parts in films and television and stage which were not only bringing in good money but giving him a good reputation. Then he played Jesus Christ in an old medieval play which was filmed for television. The supporting cast boasted such names as Rupert Davies, Edward Woodward, Ewen Solon, and Patrick Troughton. The performance was much admired, and Charles Houston received a crop of excellent notices and then his career, instead of flowering, took a sudden nose dive. The television offers suddenly stopped and three very important films in which he had good parts were all canceled—the ill-fated *Cleopatra* was one of them. *He did not work for eighteen months.* It will be remembered that Jeffrey Hunter, who played the part in a long-since-forgotten epic *King of Kings*, died shortly after, and that Warner Baxter's career went into a decline after he played it in a famous silent version in the late twenties. As for *Jesus Christ Superstar*, it is not known whether this comes under this particular superstition. Perhaps a modern rock musical doesn't count, or maybe music has the power to take away the curse. Time alone will tell.

If there is an unlucky film, then it must surely be *The Exorcist*, though confirmation of this idea will have to wait until there is a remake. The subject might well have caused alarm for the religious and the nervous, for it is the only film to date that deals with deadly seriousness and accuracy with the theme of diabolical possession and, in the process, spares the audience no physical detail, however repulsive. Its history would have made Dracula smile; it was reported that everybody in the film was ill at some time, that the sets were all destroyed by fire involving cripplingly expensive rebuilding, that Jack Magowran, the Irish actor, who played the sarcastic film producer, died of a heart attack before they could film his death scene in the film, and that the skeptical director, William Friedkin, was finally converted to a belief in the

THREE

Theatrical Ghosts

The English theatres are happily well populated with ghosts, for these old, creaking buildings provide the right atmosphere for their activities and a comfortable and suitable home for them. Most of these ghosts are benevolent, pleased to see visitors, and view with apparent approval the entertainments and developments that they could never have anticipated in their lifetime, though it is interesting to speculate what the ghost of Mrs. Siddons would think of *Oh! Calcutta!* or the ghost of Charles Kean of *Oklahoma*. Without doubt, the oldest ghost, the most famous, the most frequently seen and consequently the best documented is in the Theatre Royal, Drury Lane (known affectionately as the "Lane" to theatregoers). The ghost is known as The Man in Grey, and it must be stated firmly that he had no connection with Lady Eleanor Smith's famous Regency novelette, nor with the delightful and very successful film of the same name.

The Man in Grey has one curious habit which places him in a very different category from most other ghosts: he is a daytime ghost and only appears in the morning and afternoon. In addition he confines his activities to the upper circle; he appears at one end, goes through the bar at the rear, walks along the back of the circle, and then vanishes into the opposite wall. During the rehearsals of a new show, he has occasionally been seen sitting down or standing at the rim, gazing down at the stage, a silent, immobile gray figure. He has even been known to appear at matinees with an audience present. On these occasions not everybody sees him. Some do and some don't according to whether or not they're receptive to psychic phenomena. He has been seen by cleaners, attendants, barmen, and various members of the theatre staff.

Most people do not realize that he is a ghost and assume that he is one of the actors or perhaps a costumed attendant, but if people go to the upper circle in the hope and expectation of seeing him, then he will not appear. Royal visits from the queen, visits from TV companies doing a documentary of the theatre, radio writers, journalists, and members of the Society for Psychical Research, all these are doomed to disappointment. The Man in Grey, though not shy of people, dislikes publicity and is no respecter of royalty.

Nobody knows who he is or anything about him. Was he an actor? On the grounds of probability it is thought he probably was not, for ghosts tend to haunt the place where they spent their lives and what is an actor doing spending his time in an upper circle? There is a theory that he was a young man-about-town who was in love with one of the actresses, spent his time watching her from the circle, antagonized her lover or her husband, and was killed in a duel. For over two hundred years he has been seen, and in 1850 there was a discovery which cast an interesting light on the matter. The theatre was being altered to accommodate more seats and a group of workmen knocking down the right-hand wall of the circle found a little chamber. What they saw was worthy of any novel set in Regency times and a good example of life following literature. There was a skeleton (male)

The most striking of these, in both senses of the word, is a gentleman (one presumes it is a gentleman, though with ghosts one can never be sure) who has never yet been seen but is tangible. Very tangible indeed. He is clearly a former actor because he confines his activities to the stage and the dressing rooms and contrives to make his presence felt in many different ways. On first nights he goes to the dressing rooms and helps the suffering actors on with their clothes. Many such, struggling with recalcitrant cloaks, buttons, zippers, and dresses, have felt a pair of hands help them. Buttons and zippers are efficiently done up, coats and jackets are gently placed on shoulders, dresses tied and ribboned at the back.

In every case the actor or actress says "thank you" to what he or she imagines is the dresser and turns around to find the dressing room empty. The experience, they have all firmly stated, is a little puzzling but not frightening. The ghost produces an atmosphere of friendliness and affection. In the wings, they stand shivering nervously, waiting for the entrance. Suddenly they feel a reassuring pat on the back or a kiss on the neck. They turn round to acknowledge this gesture to find nobody there. The ghost clearly knows what we all go through on first nights and is anxious to help in any possible way. But his help is not limited to off-stage. Betty Jo Jones, the American actress, who was in the original *Oklahoma* company in 1947, told the theatre's publicity director, W. Macqueen Pope, that one evening she was playing a small scene upstage. It was a comedy scene, she was young and inexperienced, and, in addition, the wide-open spaces of the Drury Lane are death to comedy. Suddenly she felt a pair of hands grip her and steer her, firmly but gently, down to the footlights. This is where she was forced to play out her scene, much to the bewilderment of the others on the stage. She was later asked for an explanation, but nobody believed her when she told them what had actually happened. The second night the same thing happened. She was standing upstage, ready to start her small comedy scene, when the hands propelled her down to the footlights, and the scene which had been coldly received started to get laughter. The following night it happened again, and with the confidence born of experience, she played her scene and was rewarded with a round of applause. From then on she invariably played that particular scene downstage with great success, and the unseen hands were never felt again.

According to W. Macqueen Pope in his book *Pillars of Drury Lane*, an actress, Doreen Duke, experienced the unseen hands but over a much longer period of time. She felt them when she stepped onto the empty stage to audition for a part in *The King and I*. The hands were gentle and reassuring; her nerves vanished, she gave a good audition and got the part. Throughout the rehearsals the hands were in evidence, patting and stroking her in moments of tension, and on the first night they were there, too, giving her reassurance when she most needed it.

It is not that his activities are always so benevolent. Occasionally he kicks actors in the seat of their trousers and quite violently, sometimes in the wings, sometimes even on the stage. This seems to be confined to bad actors, or good actors giving bad performances when miscast, which isn't quite the same thing. This happened to Mr. Beerbohm Tree in the nineties when he was giving a soliloquy from *Falstaff* at a Shakespearean gala matinee at Drury Lane. The kick was felt, and furthermore seen to be felt by a packed, royalty-studded audience, though it must be admitted that the sweating Mr. Tree cleverly passed it off as part of the performance, a brilliant piece of comic mime. The incident was later reported to Sir Henry Irving that the Drury Lane ghost had kicked Mr. Tree during his *Falstaff* soliloquy. "That settles it," said Sir Henry with gleeful sarcasm, "The ghost isn't an actor, he's a critic!"

The ghost has had many further moments of mischief. Tony Britton, who appeared in the 1973 production of *No No Nanette*, remembers a couple of amusing incidents: "I actually had the tail of my jacket pulled when on stage, and the other night he goosed a chorus girl within a few feet of where I was standing, and it wasn't me, honest!" Gloria Stuart of the *Oklahoma* company remembers that one Friday night when she had been paid she locked the money into a drawer in her dressing-room table, and locked the room before going onto the stage. She was absent for fifteen minutes with both keys in her pocket. When she returned after the performance, the drawer was still locked but the money had gone. She searched the dressing room high and low and then fetched the company manager. Together they searched the dressing room again, and then the money was discovered—in her handbag. Nobody could have got in, it was clearly not the work of mortal man, so it just had to be the ghost up to his tricks again. It was reported to Harry Price, ghost watcher extraordinary, who promised to investigate, saying that it was clearly a case of psychic transference, a familiar trick with poltergeists, if poltergeists it was.

Who is he? Who is the actor who knows about the art of comedy, is kind to beginners, and has a violent and mischievous sense of humor? Experts have considered the matter and the most popular theory is Joseph Grimaldi, the most loved and the most successful comic of the Regency period, whose great career centered round the Drury Lane. He would certainly have administered punishment to a posturing actor; he would certainly have steered a talented but inexperienced young girl to a favorable position; he would certainly have hidden a pay packet. He would certainly have goosed a chorus girl.

Other ghosts have been seen in the theatre. In 1900 two elderly ladies were sitting in two gangway stalls during a sparsely attended matinee. They noticed an old man sitting at the end of the row next to the wall. He was dressed in early nineteenth-century clothes, had white hair and a square white face. Their attention was distracted by the play, and when they looked back he had vanished. This startled them because he had not passed them, nor could he have climbed over the seats to the exit, and there was no other way. Later they compared their memories with a portrait in the Garrick Club—it was Charles Kean, who had died thirty years earlier.

In 1937 an actor, Clifford Heatherley, appeared briefly as Henry VIII's ghost in Ivor Novello's third musical *Crest of the Wave*. Soon after the opening he died during a mid-week matinee, and instructions were given that, until a replacement was found, the short scene would be cut. That night the ghost of Henry VIII did appear and it was not the understudy. The horrified and astonished company were prepared to swear that it was Clifford Heatherley himself. In 1960 during the run of *Camelot*, Elizabeth Larner returned to her dressing room during the intermission to find a tall stately lady sitting in the armchair. She assumed it was a new dresser, but when the lady rose and revealed that she was wearing a dark eighteenth-century dress and cloak and then proceeded to vanish through the wall, she realized that it wasn't. Her description tallied with a portrait in the theatre greenroom; it was Mrs. Siddons, whose uniquely distinguished career as London's greatest tragedienne had centered round the Lane.

Another ghost lives in the Haymarket Theatre Royal. This is one of the most beautiful theatres in the world, old, atmospheric, rich in tradition and success, full of long, creaking, wooden corridors, concealed doorways, a warren of carpeted staircases leading to hidden offices and dressing rooms, a unique and enchanting theatre where it is a pleasure and privilege to play and work. The ghost is seldom seen. He opens and shuts doors. He walks up and down the corridors when the theatre is empty. He will sometimes cast a shadow as he walks. He will sometimes enter the dressing room on the stage level and sit down and just gaze at the occupant who might be resting, entertaining his friends, or preparing for the play. Peter Barkworth, who occupied dressing-room number one which has a connecting door onto the stage (no longer used), felt an unseen presence on a number of occasions when he was resting between the performances after a midweek matinee. It was decidedly eerie when he rested with the lights out, so he always kept them on. Others who have had this room have stated that on occasions they felt that someone was in the room watching them.

The ghost is Mr. John Buckstone, longtime manager of the theatre from 1853 to 1878. He was Queen Victoria's favorite manager, as the Haymarket was her favorite theatre. Many times he sat with her in her royal box, and the first recorded appearance after his death was in 1880 when he was seen sitting in the royal box. Many people during the last century have seen him: firemen, stage-door keepers, cleaners, and concessionaires. The experience of a wardrobe mistress can be taken as typical. The play was *Hadrian VII*, with actors dressed up as cardinals and the pope and other colorful characters. One evening the wardrobe mistress was ironing in her room and she heard a knock. "Come in and sit down, dear," she said, "shan't be a moment." She assumed it was an actor come to fetch a piece of his costume and was a little surprised when there was no answer. She turned round and there was a man in mid-Victorian costume which was not the period of the play. "What are you wearing?" she said. "What's this all about?" The man turned and smiled and then moved away out of her sight, and when she looked out into the corridor, it was empty. Later, she was drinking in the Buckstone Club, an actors' club in the basement of a house opposite the stage door. Hanging on the wall was a large engraving of the man she had seen. The resemblance was startling. It was Mr. Buckstone.

The ghost of Mr. Buckstone is above all a friendly ghost, and Peter Underwood, who has gathered a great deal of colorful information on the subject in his book *Haunted London*, is of the opinion that happiness and love over a long period of time in life can produce a ghost after death, as is clearly the case here. Mr. Buckstone loved his theatre, and was greatly loved by his actors, many of whom have had very kind things to say about him in their memoirs and reminiscences. Mrs. Stuart Watson, the present chairman and managing director, has an office which used to be Buckstone's dressing room. It is here that the feeling of his presence is strongest: his footsteps on the carpet, his opening the door, and occasionally his hand to rummage about a cupboard or to turn the pages of a book which was once his. "I'm no longer frightened of him," she has said to inquirers. "He was happy here and if I feel he's in the room I'll make him welcome. I wouldn't want anything to hurt or scare him."

The ghost of William Terriss haunts London's Adelphi Theatre in the Strand. He was the darling of the late Victorian theatre, a handsome, charming lively actor who had learned his trade in Irving's company at the Lyceum and had enjoyed a highly privileged position there. Irving was very fond of him and allowed familiarities and impertinencies from him which were unthinkable from anybody else. Ellen Terry, in her letters to Shaw, said that "Terriss could do no wrong, the Chief lets him get away with anything." There was one occasion illustrating this, which was told and retold throughout London's clubs and greenrooms—the night he stole Irving's limelight. In those star-ridden and totally undemocratic days, the star actor performed in the unwinking glare of an individual spotlight which followed him round and concentrated on him even if he was doing nothing, while the supporting company would act themselves into a stupor in the dim twilight around him. The supporting company would grumble, but the custom was sanctioned by centuries of theatrical tradition and there was really nothing they could do about it.

Terriss thought otherwise. He went to Irving and asked if he could have a spot once in a while. Irving refused. Terriss renewed his request. Irving refused again. The defeat rankled and one evening he took action. The play that night was *Louis XI*, a mindless melodrama by one of Irving's tame poets, whose worthlessness was redeemed only by Irving's extraordinarily malevolent performance of the evil, hunchbacked king (a dry run for his famous Richard III) and the riveting death scene which ended the play. Terriss, in the small part of Louis's bastard son and successor, was doomed to stand motionless by the deathbed while Irving writhed and groaned and screeched in his death agonies. One evening he went to the light operator. "The Guvnor says to put the spot on me," he said. The man was incredulous. Such a thing had never happened in all his years at the Lyceum, but Terriss, who was nothing if not persuasive, eventually convinced him that the order had indeed come from Irving. That night Irving played his death agonies in darkness while Terriss, registering nameless emotions, stood bathed in light and enjoyed himself hugely. Af-

*The Adelphi Theatre in London is haunted by its former
actor-manager, William Terriss*

terward, the storm broke. Terriss, his guilt established, was summoned to number one dressing room for either a severe reprimand or dismissal or possibly both. In fact he got neither. Accurately assessing the situation, he flung his arms open and assumed an expression of deep contrition. "I'm sorry, Guvnor," he said, "but you see, it was the only chance I had!" It was a crafty piece of flattery, for the implied compliment was not lost on Irving, who smiled and relaxed. "Don't do it again, m'boy," was his answer and with that the incident was closed.

A few years later, in 1890, Terriss left the Lyceum and went into management on his own. He took a lease on the Adelphi and launched a season of popular romances and melodramas. Seven years of financial success and popular acclaim followed. The girls and middle-aged women welcomed his arrival on the scene of the commercial theatre, and although the term was not to be invented for another twenty years, he was, in fact, the first unofficial matinee idol. He was also a very good actor, critics liked him, and older theatregoers, while sometimes shaking gray heads over his choice of plays, responded to his charm and personality.

In 1897 he presented a melodramatic thriller, *Secret Service*. In the company was an actor called Richard Prince, who was that very sad person, a very bad actor who believed himself to be a very good one. His status in the company was a humble one, little more than a walk-on with a couple of unimportant lines, but he fancied himself in the leading part and considered himself better than Terriss. He even learned it and asked permission to understudy it, but the company manager sensibly decided that he was not good enough even for this. One day he might have to play it, and the public deserved something for their money. The rejection hurt Prince very much and he began to brood miserably. This is where the situation took a very unhappy turn. He confided his feelings to his fellow actors. He told them that he was a great actor and that he should be playing the star part and that he felt that only Terriss' obstinacy stood in his way of success.

His colleagues, with unbelievable cruelty and thoughtlessness, encouraged his delusions and even added to them. Terriss was jealous, they said. He knew that Prince was a better actor and he was scared of giving him his chance for fear that his own status might be imperiled. If it wasn't for Terriss, he, Prince, would be a star, and girls would queue up for his autograph and he, too, would be invited to dine with royalty and he would have his photo in front of the theatre. In dressing room and pub they talked to him and fed his self-pitying fantasies. Doubtless they considered it a huge joke, and in all fairness to them (their names are happily unknown, for the responsibility for what happened is largely theirs), they did not intend it to be taken seriously and could have had no possible suspicion of the effect it was having on the unhappy Prince nor of its outcome. The psychological torture continued week after week. Nightly, Terriss received his standing ovation and nightly Prince writhed in jealous fury in the wings, watching the charlatan and impostor (as he had privately denounced him) receive the applause to which he was not entitled.

The situation was aggravated because Terriss was totally unaware of Prince's feelings. Terriss, like all the actor-managers of the day, looked after his company with a benevolent paternalism. He sent them presents on birthdays and wedding anniversaries, took them out for supper and preperformance drinks, chatted to them amiably in the wings, and made it clear that he regarded them as friends and not merely employees. Prince was no exception. Terriss sent him a birthday card, invited him out to supper at Rules, and even invited him with a couple of others to Sunday lunch at home. From Prince's point of view, it was insufferable that he should endure such patronage.

It was the night of Friday, December 16, 1897. Terriss had been enjoying his usual preperformance pint of champagne and dozen oysters at Rules with Seymour Hicks, who had married his daughter Ellaline and was appearing in *The Gaiety Girl* at the Gaiety Theatre opposite the Adelphi. They parted for their respective theatres at seven, Seymour Hicks down the alleyway to the

Strand and Terriss along the dimly lit Maiden Lane to the stage door of the Adelphi. Just before he reached it, Prince leaped at him and stabbed three times with a knife which he had, it was later established, bought only that afternoon. Terriss sank to the ground bleeding profusely from a chest wound and was carried inside to his dressing room by the theatre staff. Seymour Hicks, hearing shouts and screams, ran back, heard the news, rushed inside the theatre to find his father-in-law lying on the couch with his leading lady, Jessie Milward, weeping loudly and cradling the dying man in her arms. Just before he died he was heard to whisper, "I shall come back," and a minute later, "Can any man be so foolish as to believe that there is no afterlife?"

Prince had remained at the stage door, laughing maniacally and flourishing his knife. The police arrived and had no trouble in seizing him and dragging him, still screaming obscenities, off to Bow Street Police Station round the corner. He was tried, found guilty of willful murder, and since he was clearly insane, sent to Broadmoor Criminal Lunatic Asylum. By a curious twist of fate, the theatrical success he so keenly desired was later achieved, for he became the leading light of the prison drama group, and among the plays which he presented and starred in was *Secret Service*. Throughout his forty years of imprisonment, he never gave any trouble, and died in 1937 at the age of eight-one, greatly mourned by his fellow inmates.

During the following years, a great many strange things happened at the Adelphi. The ghost of Terriss kept his word and did come back, not once but many times. Many people have seen the tall, well-dressed man in frock coat and top hat with walking stick stand outside the stage door, walk through and down the corridors, pass through the locked door into the dressing room which he formerly occupied. The stagehands see him standing in the wings, the electricians see him walk across the footlights into the empty auditorium, the ushers see him go through the empty lobby into the street. He never does anything, he never speaks or even stops. He just passes by and vanishes. Inevitably, it is assumed that he is a member of the company, or a member of the theatre staff with old-fashioned tastes in clothes. Only when they see a photo of Terriss do they recognize him, or when they inquire from older members of the theatre staff who then tell them who it is. Various disturbing occult happenings have been reported . . . lights that come up and down, changes in temperature from very hot to very cold within the space of a single minute, green lights hovering about dressing-room tables, and a lift that behaves in a very peculiar manner when nobody is in it.

More disturbing is the behavior of the couch in Terriss' former dressing room which has been known to bump up and down, to roam round the room while strange footsteps and rappings are heard in the empty corridor. More than one leading lady occupying dressing room number one has experienced these alarming things. But most disturbing of all is the appearance of Terriss on the platform of Charing Cross Underground Station where in his lifetime he would frequently wait for a train, after a convivial meal at Rules, the last train which was in those days considerably later than it is now.

From time to time various peculiar occult incidents are reported and discussed in pub, club, and greenroom. Hersey Pigot, a well-known West End dresser, once worked at the Piccadilly Theatre in 1970, dressing Sarah Miles who was playing Mary Queen of Scots in her husband's play, *Vivat, Vivat Regina*. There was a series of beautiful and dazzling costumes and one very quick change, from a cream-and-red creation to a dark brown riding habit. Three people were involved in this change which had to be done in slightly under a minute. To make it possible, Hersey used to unbutton it in advance, and before she left the theatre at night, put it thus in the wardrobe in Sarah Miles' dressing room. One night, when the quick change came, she discovered to her annoyance that the buttons were done up. The change took a little longer that evening. Hersey inquired angrily round the stage staff, but nobody knew anything about it.

The following night it happened again. Suspicion naturally fell on the cleaners, but they too denied all knowledge. That night she and Sarah Miles placed the unbuttoned dress into the wardrobe, locked it and then the dressing room, and took both keys with them. Nobody could have gone in, but nevertheless the dress was buttoned up as usual when they arrived at the theatre the following evening. Clearly something supernatural was in the air, but what? Or who? Sarah Miles had a sad theory. "It must be the ghost of Mary Queen of Scots haunting me," she said, laughing. "Perhaps she doesn't like the play—or my performance." This aggravation continued for a week and then ended and there was no further trouble.

Another piece of clothing that provided a rather more disturbing occult experience turned up at the Duke of York's Theatre during the run of a play called *The Queen Came By*. It was a little black bolero jacket originally made for a production of *Charley's Aunt* before World War I and hired from one of the big West End costumers. It became known as The Strangler, and there was undoubtedly a curse on it. A number of women in the company wore it in their turn, and each time there was unpleasantness. First, the play's star, Thora Hird, complained that it was too tight, even though it had been comfortable at the original fitting, and that it became tighter every time she wore it. Three other women wore it, and all of them experienced not only a feeling of tightness and suffocation, but also a sensation of fear and trembling, as if something exceedingly nasty was about to happen to them. These feelings vanished the minute they took it off. A fourth, Mrs. Frederick Piffard, wife of the producer, discovered to her alarm that she had red weals all over her throat, as if somebody had been trying to strangle her.

The matter was reported to occult-minded friends who arranged to have a séance inside the theatre with the jacket placed before them. The mystery was solved. From the proceedings, a clear picture of the terrible events emerged. The jacket, it seemed, had originally belonged to a young actress who had aroused the jealous hostility of her boy friend. He had attacked her in the theatre one evening, strangled her, placed her body in a barrel, and thrown it into the river, another remarkable example of how evil lives on after death not only in places and people but also in objects. Peter Underwood, whose well-researched book *Haunted London* is probably the definitive treatment of the subject, discovered that the jacket subsequently became the property of a California gentleman named Lloyd. He, his wife, their daughter, and a number of others all tried on the jacket, and all of them felt faint, frightened, and strangled.

No less alarming was the incident at the Theatre Royal, Margate, a late eighteenth-century gem and one of the oldest theatres in England. Bernard Archard recalls acting in a play there, supposedly a comedy. He remembers that there was one particular spot which he and his colleague in the scene thought was very funny, but they never got a laugh. Nightly, they would try different inflections, different facial expressions, different bits of supporting business. All useless. The audience obstinately refused to laugh. One evening, in desperation, they decided to stay behind after the performance for an extra rehearsal. Privacy was essential, so when the company had gone home, they searched everywhere to check that there was nobody around and locked up the theatre so no one could sneak in, and then went onto the stage. By the light of a single working bulb which cast eerie shadows on the bare wooden boards, they ran the scene. When Bernard Archard said the line, with an entirely new inflection he'd just thought of, a loud and long laugh suddenly echoed throughout the theatre from somebody, apparently, seated in the front of the dress circle. "The effect was indescribably frightening," he later said. "We dropped everything and ran to the circle, but there was nobody there. We searched the theatre from top to bottom, but it was empty and all the doors were locked." Considerably shaken by the incident, they decided to abandon the rehearsal and went home. The following evening the recalcitrant lines did get a laugh, a very good one, and so they continued to do every night they played the comedy. Supernatural approval of his comedy timing had clearly given Bernard Archard the confidence he needed, but who was it who laughed?

The popular theory is that it must have been the ghost of Sarah Thorne, the elderly Victorian matriarch who managed the theatre for a period of years in the mid-nineteenth century and who also founded a drama school. Many people working there have seen a dim gray figure glide down a corridor, or stand in the corner of what is now the dress-circle bar but which used to be her office. The gaunt acquiline features they can dimly see match up neatly with the portrait of her in the theatre lobby.

The odd behavior of the theatre lights has also been laid at her door. One evening in the middle fifties, Stanley Mills, the stage manager, locked up the dress circle where the lighting switchboard was kept, locked up the theatre, and went home. In the small hours of the morning the police summoned him. It seemed that the front and back doors of the theatre were wide open and the theatre was flooded with light. On investigation it was discovered that, although the light switches had all been turned down to on, the door of the lighting switchboard was still locked. It was all very strange, and it was generally decided that a supernatural or occult force was the only explanation.

Sarah Thorne had certainly chosen a very suitable venue for her activities and her perambulations as I discovered when I played there for a season of weekly rep in the winter of 1954. It had a truly delightful atmosphere where any ghost would feel at home . . . creaking wooden corridors, a crazy, crumbling attic, accessible by a ladder, which was my dressing room, cobweb-filled cellars, a warren of rooms, passages, and unexpected little nooks and niches weaving their tortuous way round the theatre. One afternoon I came early to the theatre. There was an excellent Bechstein piano in the pit, and I wanted to make a little music and thus put myself into the right mood for that evening's performance of *Ring Round the Moon*. I changed into the Butterfly Collector's check suit and went to the pit and started to play. I remember that I started with the D flat Etude of Liszt and followed this with a Schubert Impromptu. Then I started to play the E major study of Chopin, the popular one which is (regrettably) known to some as a wartime pop tune under the title of "So Deep Is the Night."

I had played a few bars, and suddenly the temperature, which had been cool but not cold, suddenly became very cold indeed. It was as if somebody had opened a door on a freezing night. I looked round but all the doors were closed, and in any case it was a fine spring day. Shivering, but unsuspicious, I continued to play. Then I heard a voice saying very quietly just behind me, "No, not that." I turned round very quickly, but there was nobody there. The stalls were empty. I looked nervously around, but there was no sign of anybody. I shrugged my shoulders, thinking I must have imagined it and continued to play the same piece. Suddenly the temperature dropped even lower and I started to shiver and I had the strongest feeling that somebody was standing right behind me. I began to feel frightened and then I heard the voice again saying, with a touch of real urgency, "No!" Once again I turned round and once again there was nobody, but this time I distinctly saw a formless, shapeless light hovering over the stalls about ten feet away from me. I was too frightened to run away or make any move; I just stood there shivering, my eyes glued onto this shapeless dim light. Then the idea suddenly came into my head that I was in danger unless I started to play again and something different. By a supreme effort of will I forced myself to sit down at the piano and I started to play, this time the second movement of the *Pathétique* sonata. It was a happy choice, for within the space of half a minute the temperature not only returned to normal but actually became warmer than it had been, as if somebody had switched on the heating. I stopped trembling, my feelings of fear vanished and were replaced by a surge of happiness and pleasure. I finished the movement and then looked round. The light had vanished, the presence had gone, but did I hear, or did I only *imagine* I heard, a soft voice saying, "Thank you."

I can offer no sensible explanation for all this. Whether this was the ghost of Sarah Thorne or not is a matter for speculation, but for lack of any other claimant (and none has been seen or felt), she must take the responsibility. From this, one gathers that she liked Beethoven and hated Chopin, but why this tender, lyrical piece should have aroused such fierce emotions, it is impossible to say. Perhaps in her lifetime she associated it with the death of somebody close to her, or some tragedy in the theatre. Maybe it was used in a play which had been a disastrous failure. This can affect one for life. To this day, and for that reason, I can't listen to the overture to *The Force of Destiny* without shuddering. Or maybe she herself was playing it when something terrible happened. Whatever the reason, the piece seems to have a definite curse on it inside the theatre, and while I was there I never touched the piano again.

The ghost of Ivor Novello is supposed to haunt the Palace Theatre, London. This is where his last musical *King's Rhapsody* was playing when he died of a heart attack in 1951, and the theatre is always associated with his memory. Nobody claims to have actually seen him, but his spirit has been felt, as when a young actress recently auditioning for a part in *Jesus Christ Superstar* prayed out loud to him as she stood trembling in the wings. Her reward was not only to get the part of Mary but also Novello's dressing room.

Sir Alec Guinness was supposed to have seen the ghost of Shakespeare sitting in the stalls on the first night of his ill-starred 1951 *Hamlet*, who supposedly got up and walked out in the middle of the performance. The press played this story up in a big way and it has since appeared in magazines and books dealing with the occult. I wrote to Sir Alec for confirmation and discovered from him that the whole story rose from a little misunderstanding. What he had said to his fellow actors in the interval was not that he had seen Shakespeare get up and leave but that he had seen somebody who looked like Shakespeare. The mysterious stranger, in fact, turned out later to be Somerset Maugham.

The ghost of Dylan Thomas has recently been seen at the Bush Theatre. This is a little fringe theatre formerly a BBC rehearsal room and it occupies premises above the Shepherds Bush Hotel.

A documentary play about Thomas was being rehearsed by the author-actor Michael Mundell and six colleagues. One evening after a late-night rehearsal, they locked up and remembered that they had been observed by a man who had stood silently at the back of the theatre. They went back to fetch him but he wasn't there and there was no trace of him anywhere and all the exit doors were locked. He was described later as plump, podgy-faced, about forty, and with dark curly hair, a description that perfectly fitted the Welsh poet. It was remembered that the Shepherds Bush Hotel was where Thomas used to go regularly for his drinks after working at Lime Grove Television Studios round the corner.

American theatres don't provide such happy homes for ghosts, as they are all much newer, the oldest being Ford's Theatre in Washington, little more than a hundred years old, where Abraham Lincoln was shot. Nevertheless, a few ghosts do survive into the twentieth century. The Belasco is undoubtedly haunted by the ghost of its namesake and creator, David Belasco, that supreme arch-poseur who decorated his room like a monastery and habitually wore a monk's habit. Actors from time to time have seen him sitting in his favorite stage box, dimly visible behind the curtains, his white hair, bald head, and monk's cowl easily recognizable. And at eleven o'clock at night, when the theatre is empty, the elevator can be heard whirring and creeping its way up to his rooms at the top of the theatre. Yet the elevator is lying at the bottom of the shaft, its cable long since snapped, rusty and immobile. At night when nobody is there, laughter can be heard, singing, footsteps, doors opening and shutting and—most eerily of all—the front curtain mysteriously raises, hovers, and then lowers.

A number of other rather sinister happenings have been recorded. From time to time, the ghost of a tightrope walker can be seen in the Palace Theatre in New York, swinging away from the dress-circle rim. People watching through the peephole in the curtain, before the audience is admitted, have seen him, seen the death fall, and heard a shrill cry of pain and fear. It happened in the 1950s. His name was Louis Borsalino, part of a vaudeville acrobat team called "The Four Casting Pearls." He was taken to the hospital and died shortly after. The tragedy cast a distinct gloom over the theatre thereafter, and it is regarded, understandably, as a sign of very bad luck if you see his ghost or hear the ghostly death scream.

Jay Fox, director and choreographer, has recorded a very peculiar occult experience. A few summers ago he was setting up a musical version of the life of Harry Houdini. From the start, he remembers, everything went wrong; there were money problems, backers backed in and then backed out. Casting problems abounded, with the right people accepting and then walking out in favor of better paid jobs, plus the perennial difficulty of finding performers who could sing, dance, and act all equally well. There were script problems, with a long, complex life to be honed down into a two-and-a-half-hour show, plus technical problems of how to put on the stage, without too much risk to the star, all the terrifying feats which Houdini actually performed. The early rehearsals took place in a little theatre in the country and these were hectic, traumatic days. One day it was suggested that they use a Ouija board to see if they could establish some sort of contact with the Fates, and find out if there was any help they could get from the other world. They did so, and the message came back loud and clear, "I'll send a sign." After the depression and gloom this lifted their spirits and rehearsals continued in a spirit of optimism.

One evening they decided to decorate the outside of the theatre with strips of tinfoil. A wind came along, and from nowhere, which mystified them, for it was a sunny day. The strips of tinfoil were rearranged and to their astonished eyes began to form themselves into the shape of a big *H*. Houdini. Harry Houdini was trying to get in touch and trying to tell them that everything was going to be all right and that he was taking a personal interest in the project. The opening performances took place in a private house called Wheatleigh, owned by a lady, Stephanie Barber. During the performances, a trunk used for Houdini's escape suddenly revealed a large *H* painted on the front. It had not been there before and nobody had any idea who had done it. Another sign. The performances were a great success and made considerable money, though, unhappily, it has not yet arrived on Broadway.

The old Met was a house which attracted every sort of human excess as an international opera house rightly should, and it should, and did, provide the right atmosphere for a ghost. During the final years of that wonderful old echoing gilded house, there was a stately old dowager who occupied a seat in the parterre. She sat at the end of the row and provided an endless distraction for her immediate neighbors by loud tut-tuts of disapproval, shakes of her bejeweled hands, clucking and audible comments of disparagement whenever the current soprano was singing an aria. She invariably vanished after the first act, never to reappear until the next evening. One evening a woman sitting nearby became seriously annoyed. Her attempts to quiet the woman were unsuccessful, so she went to the head usher and reported the facts to him. The head usher was deeply embarrassed and was unable to suggest a satisfactory method of dealing with the nuisance, whereupon one of the directors of the Met took the lady aside, bought her a glass of sherry, and explained to her in confidence that this was the ghost of the late Mme Frances Alda, the former Mrs. Gatti-Cazzaza (former director of the Met), who apparently made it a practice in her lifetime of turning up whenever any of her favorite operas were being performed for the express purpose of making life difficult for the soprano, and found she was unable to stop the habit after her death. She was seen many times by the old-time regulars of the old Met, but has not been seen in the new building in the Lincoln Center.

Fifty years ago, a woman ran down the center aisle of the Avon Theatre in Utica, New York, and shot the pipe organist dead. It

David Belasco is seen from time to time in the theatre which bears his name.

John Wilkes Booth, whose presence lingers on in Ford's Theatre

seemed that the man had been cheating on his wife and she took the time-honored way out of the problem. From then on, till its demolition just after World War II, in 1947, the theatre was haunted. Night porters would testify that the organ would rise out of the pit at midnight and play itself with no human hands on the keys. The theatre would be filled with sinister organ music which would stop as soon as somebody entered. From then onward, it was exceedingly difficult to find people to work in the theatre in any capacity. Mrs. Ruby L. Betts, who worked there shortly after the murder, is of the opinion that the whole affair could have been an elaborate practical joke on the part of the local electrician. This is true of many hauntings, so the matter remains undecided.

Abraham Lincoln was assassinated at Ford's Theatre on April 14, 1865, by a none-too-successful actor from a famous theatrical family, John Wilkes Booth. He broke into the Presidential box, emptied his gun, a Derringer, into Lincoln's head, and made his escape by leaping over the rim of the box onto the stage and running diagonally across the stage, out the stage door, and into the street.

The theatre fell into disuse a few years later and was allowed to stand empty for a whole century, a classic example of the primeval curse in action. But in 1968 the Ford's Theatre Society restored it both as a museum of assassination souvenirs and theatricalia, and partly as a working, practical theatre. Does the ghost of Booth haunt the theatre? Logically speaking, if there is a ghost, it should be Lincoln's, who was killed there, rather than his assassin, who died several miles away. Certainly there is an occult presence. Many have felt and heard it. Once again there emerges the familiar pattern of footsteps in the empty theatre, lights coming on and going off, curtains raising and lowering without human hands, strange voices laughing and crying. One stagehand was so frightened by these, while changing to go home, that he ran out into the street wearing only his underpants.

Supporters of the ghost theory find some confirmation in one rather peculiar fact. The spirit of evil definitely does survive even a century of disuse and darkness. When Booth ran zigzag across the stage, scattering terrified actors on both sides, he left behind an occult aura which has been felt. Actors standing on, or even close to, this occult line have been affected in very definite and disturbing ways. They feel sick and nervous; they tremble; they forget their lines; they even forget where they are and what play they are doing. Hal Holbrook, performing his famous Mark Twain recital, and Jack Aronson in an evening of Herman Melville, have both testified to a sudden and terrifying drop of temperature as they crossed the line of evil. A photo of the empty theatre taken by Matthew Brady just after the assassination reveals a transparent figure standing inside the Presidential box. Pamela M. Larratt, who has recounted these enthralling facts in the *Players Club* magazine, says: "To the show business end of the theater, the suggestible horror of it all seems a welcome idea. To the untheatrical the question of Booth's ghost is something they don't want to contemplate."

The strangest occult experience in the annals of Broadway happened to Guthrie McClintic. He has described it with a wealth of colorful and circumstantial detail in his excellent memoirs. The facts are simply as follows: he was a starving young actor in 1909 who had left his home and family in Seattle to take up a theatrical career against the wishes of his father, a man who was as strict in his outlook and prejudices as Mr. Edward Moulton-Barrett, a gentleman who was to play a not unimportant part in McClintic's later life. He enrolled in the New York Academy of Dramatic Arts and found excessively cheap lodgings at $3.50 weekly in the apartment of a Texan gentlewoman, Mrs. Heinsohn.

When he finished his course, he embarked on a long period of further training—being out of work, continually frustrated and nearly starving, a familiar and indispensable part of an actor's experience. With him it was a little worse than with some; he worked only five weeks in the first year, which is a very low figure even for 1909. The two productions he was in toured briefly but didn't get to Broadway, another familiar story. One day he was sitting in Central Park feeling very sorry for himself when he learned from another youthful actor in similar circumstances that the great Winthrop Ames was casting for a new musical, *Prunella.* Ames was then at the height of his fame as Broadway's richest, busiest, and most powerful producer, and to work with him was regarded not only as a privilege but also as a lifelong meal ticket. He went without further delay to the Ames office, only to learn that the great man was out of town, but that his manager, Mr. Foster Platt, would deal with applicants in his place. Platt was a tall, thin, forbidding personality who took a sadistic relish in intimidating the young actors who appeared before him. The interview was bleak and embarrassing and unsuccessful. Platt said that there was nothing he could offer and indicated that the meeting was over. McClintic was shaking with nerves and confusion as he stood up and in attempting to shake hands he accidentally knocked over a bottle of ink which spilled all over the desk. "Get out, Mr. McClintic," shouted Platt in a cold fury. "Get out at once!" Out McClintic went, trembling in distress and mortification. He went to a nearby hotel, sat down in the lobby, and without thinking of the possible consequences, he wrote an angry letter to the absent Winthrop Ames. He was in a fighting mood; the letter, as he later recalled, was a masterpiece of invective. He accused Ames of treating his actors badly, of neglecting young American talent in favor of foreigners (Ames's pro-British policies were notorious on Broadway), and of employing ill-mannered underlings like Mr. Foster Platt. As a postscript he offered his services and generously dwelt on his views on theatrical production. When he had written the letter, which covered several pages, his temper had cooled off considerably, and he decided not to post the letter—yet. He put it in his pocket and returned to his lodgings. When he arrived, he put the letter in a drawer and forgot all about it.

Five weeks and two dozen unsuccessful interviews later, he re-

turned home, tired and depressed, to be greeted by Mrs. Heinsohn in a state of great excitement. "Come into my room," she
said, "the table wants to speak to you." Mrs. Heinsohn had a keen
interest in the occult. She dabbled in table-rapping and spiritual-
ism and passed onto her friends what she sincerely believed to be
messages from the spirit world. That evening, the table had
rapped out McClintic's name. He went with her and the séance
began. It took a long time, but the message which the table eventually rapped out made little sense at first: "Mail that which you
have written; your entire future depends on it." What had he
written? He didn't know, he couldn't remember. And then he
realized. It was the letter still lying in a bureau drawer upstairs.
He rushed to his room, took the letter, addressed and stamped it,
ran out into the street, and posted it.

Three days later he received a letter from Winthrop Ames inviting him for an interview. The upshot was an offer to stage-
manage, at $25 weekly, a new play, *Her Own Money*, to be
directed by the ink-splattered George Foster Platt. This lead to
further engagements with Ames who finally put him on a permanent contract as his personal assistant. Fourteen months later,
with a strangely ironic twist, he found himself occupying the
same ink-splattered desk as had Mr. Foster Platt. Nearly a decade
later Ames offered him money with which to produce a play on
his own. He chose *The Dover Road* which was a huge success and
he was an independent producer. Shortly after, he married the
most beautiful, admired, and talked-of young actress, Katharine
Cornell, and thus one of the great theatrical partnerships was
formed. They moved into a beautiful house on Beekman Place
and before long he found himself one of the richest men on
Broadway. And all because of a letter written and posted in—of
all lucky years—1913.

McClintic lost touch with Mrs. Heinsohn, the unconscious
architect of his success, but she did not lose touch with him.
Once again the occult powers she possessed came to his aid. In
1932 he was attempting to produce and direct his wife in *The Bar-*

retts of Wimpole Street. The play is regarded as a modern classic, and it is difficult to realize how little faith the American theatre had in it. No less than twenty-eight Broadway producers turned it down before McClintic bought it. After a week Cornell decided that the part was not for her and asked to be released from it, and in the anxious process she went down with a bad dose of flu. It was a very tense worrying time for him, as not only his professional reputation was in the balance but a great deal of his money. He was on the verge of giving it up when a mysterious telephone call came from Mrs. Heinsohn, who had long since moved out of New York into some unspecified place in the country. "Don't worry about a thing," she said firmly, and without preliminary explanation. "You're going to have your greatest success ever," and with that she rang off. Puzzled, depressed, but hopeful, McClintic decided much against his better judgment to go ahead with the production. His better judgment turned out to be distinctly at fault, for *The Barretts of Wimpole Street* was a huge success and gave them both their greatest triumph to date. The rest is history.

The last episode in this very odd occult experience was in 1937 when McClintic was producing *Jezebel*, starring the irrepressible Tallulah Bankhead. A phone call from Mrs. Heinsohn put the whole matter into perspective. "Miss Bankhead will never play the part; you're wasting your time, and the show will be a flop. Forget it!" This time he ignored her, his better judgment telling him that even table-rapping has its limits, but once again his better judgment was at fault. Tallulah had to leave the play with a bad peritoneal infection (even her diseases were exotic; nobody had caught that since Valentino), and the part was taken over by Miriam Hopkins. It ran for a week and gave McClintic one of the few real failures of his distinguished career.

He inquired after Mrs. Heinsohn and made many attempts to find her for future reference, but he never saw her or heard from her again.

four

The Curse of *Macbeth:*
Its Origins,
Background, and History

While theatrical superstitions cover an impressively wide range of human insecurity and incredulity, not all theatre people will believe in them all, but most will believe in some, for there are superstitions to suit all tastes. There is one superstition so old, so all-consuming, so intimidating, that just about everybody in the theatre believes it, however cynical, materialistic, or hard-boiled he is—though there are a few exceptions, as will be seen later —and who can blame them for the evidence is well-nigh overwhelming and indisputable? This is the superstition about *Macbeth.*

Macbeth is the unlucky play of the theatre and has for four hundred years carried in its wake a truly terrifying trail of disaster and bad luck. The play is cursed and the curse is so strong that it is considered very unlucky to quote from it while inside a theatre. Actors are frightened even to mention it by name. If it must be discussed, and this is in itself not encouraged, then it must be done in a roundabout way, and over the years an interesting vocabulary of evasion has gained acceptance. It is talked about as "that play," or "the Scottish play," or "the unmentionable," references which must surely bewilder any backstage visitor.

The bad luck extends to anything that has ever been used for a production of *Macbeth*, and it is not unknown for an actor to refuse to wear a cloak or helmet if he learns that it was once worn in *that* play. In the old days of the traveling Shakespeare repertory companies, the scenery of the plays would be largely interchangeable, but the costumes, furniture, and settings for *Macbeth* were kept strictly apart. Never, under any circumstances, would a *Macbeth* throne be used for *King Lear* or *Othello* or *Hamlet*, however hard-pressed the manager was for money or transport or space. The bad luck also pursues the text if it is quoted in any other play: any playwright who allows his character to say, "What bloody man is this" or "When shall we three meet again?" or "Is this a dagger I see before me?" is asking for trouble and usually gets it. Unfortunately, *Macbeth* has more quotes than any other Shakespeare play. All are beautifully apt and popular and have passed into the language to the extent that many people do not realize their source.

Why should *Macbeth* be the unlucky play? It is, admittedly, a tragedy and full of blood and violence, but that is true of *King Lear*, *Othello*, *Troilus and Cressida*, *Antony and Cleopatra*, *Julius Caesar*, and *Titus Andronicus*. Macbeth is a multiple murderer, but then so is Richard III. There are ghosts, but then there are also in *Hamlet*. There are witches, but these were an acceptable ingredient of Elizabethan and Jacobean drama.

Macbeth is the murkiest, gloomiest, and most despairing of all the classical tragedies. It is a play entirely obsessed and pulsating with wickedness, and it generates such a powerful aura of evil that even to read it can make a sensitive person tremble, as Mrs. Siddons found to her cost. To see a good production of it can be a truly unnerving experience. There are evil characters in Shakespeare's other plays—Iago, Edmund, Claudius—but these are neatly offset by characters of shining virtue, Desdemona, Cordelia, Ophelia, and the plays have plenty of sunshine to lighten the darkness. But there is no sunshine in *Macbeth*. The representation of goodness in Malcolm and Lady Macduff is inept and ineffectual, because goodness was not a quality in which Shakespeare was interested while writing this play. So what is left is a tragedy which is in effect entirely black.

This is not on account of its blood and gore which can be duplicated in a dozen contemporary plays, but its particularly sinister atmosphere. And this is the point: it is the only Shakespeare play in which witchcraft and black magic and Satanism not merely play an important part, but provide the vital pivot on which the entire plot depends.

The answer lies in the circumstances in which the play was written and those of its first performance. It is thus necessary to consider briefly the state of the theatre at the turn of the sixteenth century, its relationship with its royal sovereign, and the position which Shakespeare occupied in the contemporary hierarchy.

Queen Elizabeth had been a passionate lover of all the arts, and of the theatre in particular. There can be no doubt that the flowering of the theatre in its most golden age was largely due to her enthusiasm and support, but in the last years the position had deteriorated badly. The aged queen was racked with painful diseases, tormented by unsatisfactory love affairs—the Essex disaster had cast a black cloud over her final years—plagued by affairs of state, perpetually worried by money troubles, and in no mood for theatregoing. Royal command performances, which had been so profitable and frequent, had been cut down to only three a year. Payment was £10 a performance, a sum which was considered by Shakespeare to be adequate but by no means generous.

The social status of actors was dangerously equivocal. They may have enjoyed royal patronage, but the theatre had its enemies who would have been only too happy to have closed the theatres permanently and clapped the actors into prison. The law still officially classified them as rogues and vagabonds, and if found pursuing their art they could be publicly whipped and placed in the stocks overnight. This did not often happen, but the possibility was always alarmingly there. Playwrights worked under a very severe system of censorship. Under the domination of Edward Tilney, who was master of the revels from 1579 to 1610 and thus covered the whole of Shakespeare's career, playwrights could go as far as they pleased with sex, but had to be very careful with politics and religion. Bawdy was permitted; blasphemy and sedition were not. If an author offended in either of these matters, he could be fined ten pounds, have his hand chopped off, or be sent to prison.

More disturbing for Shakespeare and his company, the artistic supremacy which he had enjoyed for so long was no longer unchallenged. There were rival companies of note, some of whom enjoyed great success and many command performances. The Admiral's Men were greatly admired, for they included in their number such shining talents as Edward Alleyn, Philip Henslowe, and Christopher Marlowe.

And then in 1603, Queen Elizabeth died and was succeeded by James VI of Scotland, son of Mary Queen of Scots. He now became James I of England, and this proved to be a decisive moment in the history of the English theatre. To explain this, it is necessary to consider the nature and personality of the new king.

His childhood and upbringing would have made a Freudian textbook. His mother was eight months' pregnant with him when she saw her lover cut to pieces before her eyes. He was an only child and suffered to the full the loneliness and misery of royal isolation. He was taken from his mother in infancy, and he never saw her again, being subsequently entrusted to a team of regents and tutors. His education was in the chilly narrow world of John Knox's bigoted hellfire religion. He grew up with a morbid interest in witchcraft and an obsessive fear of the Devil. Witchcraft was a real and ever-present social problem, and it is difficult for us in the twentieth century to understand the terror which it inspired. James knew that King Duff of Scotland had been threatened by the notorious conspiracy of the Witches of Forres; that witchcraft was responsible for the terrible storms that delayed the arrival of his bride, Princess Anne, from Denmark, and that a large number of witches had confessed to him that the Devil had incited them to do this against the foreign, ungodly princess. He knew that a terrible epidemic of witchcraft had nearly destroyed him and that hundreds of witches had been burned (over fifty were burned in England in his lifetime). The urge to tell is sometimes irresistible, and in 1595 he wrote down his thoughts on the subject and published them under the title, *Daemonologie*.

He was homosexual and his early marriage to the silly, frivolous Anne of Denmark was a purely domestic and dynastic convenience. Life was dangerous for the Stuart kings: there had been three murders in their line, and James was never entirely safe from physical violence, surrounded as he was by an aggressive and warring nobility. He grew up to be excessively squeamish of any sort of physical violence, and with a deep horror of naked steel. All his life he wore a quilted doublet to guard against the sharp thrust of the stiletto.

But this nervous, sickly, tormented, sexually divided neurotic turned out to be a passionate theatre lover. Never having seen a play, for Scotland was culturally still in the dark ages and with only the gloomy sermons of John Knox to provide popular entertainment, James was unprepared for the full impact of Shakespeare's verse, the warmth of his comedy and the color and splendor of his company's productions. He and the queen were fascinated by all they saw. They commanded endless performances until they had seen the entire Shakespearean repertoire. The company had never before been so busy traveling up and down the country to entertain the king in whatever stately home he happened to be staying.

All this had a number of material benefits and a number of long overdue improvements in the company's social and financial position now took place. In 1603 royal letters of patent were taken out. The company were now known as the King's Men, and ranked in his household as "grooms of the chamber." They were given his special protection and had a special license to perform in whatever university, town, or village they chose without hindrance or obstruction from local authorities. They were awarded a place of honor in the coronation procession and other state occasions and a special suit of clothes to wear in them. The number of command performances was increased from three a year to fifteen, and payments were doubled from £10 to £20 for each performance, with generous allowances and bonuses of up to £30 whenever they had been inconvenienced by the plague.

The accession of James I was the best thing that could have happened to Shakespeare, and it is no coincidence that the bulk of his greatest plays were all written at this time (he never wrote another comedy after *Hamlet*). Now he had financial security, popularity with the public, the respect of his colleagues and rivals, and, most important of all, a quick-witted, discriminating, and sophisticated court audience in constant attendance and expectation who could appreciate far more than the public at the Globe Theatre just what he was trying to do. Only with all this can a creative genius give of his best. Shakespeare buckled down and within five years produced *Measure for Measure*, *Othello*, *King Lear*, *Antony and Cleopatra*, *Coriolanus*, and *Macbeth*.

Macbeth was written and first performed in 1606 and although some have stated that it is an earlier play dug up for the occasion, there is enough evidence in the text to place it in this year, beyond doubt. The reference by the Witch in Act One, Scene Three to the master of the Tiger:

> A sailor's wife had chestnuts in her lap,
> And munch'd, and munch'd, and munch'd
> . . . .
> Her husband's to Aleppo gone, master of the Tiger . . .

was clearly based on a well-known nautical exploration that

caused a good deal of excitement in the summer of that year when Sir Edward Michelbourne returned on his ship *The Tiger* after a disaster-studded voyage of three years. The porter's reference to equivocation in Act Two, Scene Three,

> Faith, here's an equivocator, that could swear in both scales against either scale; who committed treason enough for God's sake, yet could not equivocate to heaven.

can only refer to the notorious execution of the Jesuit Father Garnett in the spring of 1606 who had invoked the doctrine of equivocation in his defense. The theme of royal assassination and the dialogue between Lady Macduff and her son on the subject of traitors:

> SON: What is a traitor?
> LADY M.: Why, one that swears and lies.
> SON: And be all traitors that do so?
> LADY M.: Every one that does so is a traitor, and must be hanged.
> . . . .
> SON: Who must hang them?
> LADY M.: Why, the honest men.

these are obvious references to the Gunpowder Plot which had shaken the country only the year before. In addition there are references to *Macbeth* in a number of contemporary plays published and performed a little later, *The Knight of the Burning Pestle* and *The Puritan Widow*.

So much for the date. The occasion was the state visit of the queen's brother, King Christian of Denmark, his first since his appearance at the coronation, three years earlier. The visit was to take place at the beginning of August and had been arranged in June. Suitable entertainment must be provided: Christian was known to like the theatre, and a new play was a long-standing tradition for the delight of notable foreign visitors. Sometime in early July, Shakespeare would have been summoned to the office of the comptroller in Whitehall Palace, acquainted with the facts, and asked to provide a new and suitable play for the occasion.

This commission must have given Shakespeare some considerable thought. The last royal commission he had received had been five years earlier in 1601 when Queen Elizabeth had requested a play suitable for the entertainment of the newly appointed Italian ambassador, Count Orsino. Shakespeare had very quickly concocted *Twelfth Night*, an amiable and harmless piece of romantic nonsense which had been a huge and lasting success with the court audience, partly because he had named his leading romantic hero after the guest of honor, and partly because the character of Malvolio was a shameless portrait of Sir William Knollys, Master of the Royal Household, and the most hated figure in the court. He had naturally been present at the performance and had seen with horror his alter ego, doubtless played by Burbage, costumed and made up to resemble him. During the letter scene, the court had been reduced to a hysterical uproar of delight.

But something very different would be needed for the forthcoming festivities. The Danes were reputedly very different in their tastes and outlook from the frivolous, pleasure-loving Italians, and a Scottish king was a very different thing from an English queen. James was not difficult to please, but a play written specially for him had to draw a careful line between theatricality and political discretion.

There is evidence that Shakespeare went out of his way to please his royal patron to an extent he had never done before or was to do again. The play would be set in his native Scotland and would be about a Scottish king. There would be a brief glimpse of five other Scottish kings as they paraded through the Satanic vision of the caldron. One of James's ancestors, Malcolm, would be portrayed sympathetically. Banquo, one of those supposed Stuart ancestors, would be praised with phrases like "dauntless temper of mind," and "wisdom that doth guide his valour," and there would be a number of flattering references to James's wisdom, his peace-loving intentions, and his reputedly divine powers of healing the sick. More important, the play would be short, for James did not like long plays and the royal guest did not speak or understand a word of English. James would not want to be reminded too vividly of the dangers of regicide, so the deaths of Duncan and Macbeth would take place off stage. Most important of all, the play would deal dramatically and seriously with witchcraft, the subject in which James had an obsessive, terrified interest and in which he was an acknowledged expert. And because of this, the relevant scenes, Shakespeare decided, would have to be authentic.

It was a very unfortunate decision.

In one sense the commission came at a bad time, for he was exceptionally busy in the summer of that year. There were the daily performances at the Globe and the extra performances at the weekend in the private houses. There was the complex and endless rehearsal schedule if the repertoire of up to twenty plays was to be kept up and the high standard maintained—their noble patrons were likely to request a particular play at a moment's notice and it had to be ready. And in addition to all this, he was working on his longest and most ambitious play yet, *Antony and Cleopatra*. A number of striking textual similarities make it clear that he did work on the two plays simultaneously.

He had little more than a month in which to write and rehearse it, but he was a quick worker, and the mark of the true professional is that he can produce his best work under pressure. *Macbeth* shows all the signs of having been written in a hurry. It is one of the shortest plays he wrote. There are no subplots, no superfluous characters and scenes, just the intense concentration on the one all-important theme. There are a surprising number of loose ends in the story line and one astonishing gap—why, for example, does Lady Macbeth not have her death scene? And although the white-hot inspiration carried him through to the end to produce one masterpiece that has been unfailingly popular with actors and public alike, a certain brevity and scrappiness of the scenes in the final act indicate that he was working against time.

Shakespeare would undoubtedly have done his homework well when it came to the witchcraft scenes. He would certainly have read *Daemonologie*. Like most royal writings, it is tedious and amateurish, but Shakespeare would have found it a useful pointer to the king's state of mind on the controversial subject. He would have read Reginald Scot's *Discovery of Witchcraft* published in 1584 and which caused great offense and controversy by being a spirited defense of witchcraft.

But for the actual text of the witches' scenes, Shakespeare would not have had to go further than his own memories of his boyhood in Warwickshire. Witchcraft was a very vital force in Tudor England. Shakespeare grew up in a countryside where the people lived and practiced, where they believed in witches and their powers, where they were ducked in ponds, tortured, humiliated, and killed in dreadful, unspeakable ways. He would certainly have known some in the Warwickshire villages where he lived and played. He would have heard of their spells and incantations, these being the living tradition of country life in which he grew up. In his natural and praiseworthy desire for authenticity, he went a little too far, for the witches' brew in Scene Three whose repulsive ingredients make up the potion:

> Fillet of a fenny snake,
> In the cauldron boil and bake;
> Eye of newt, and toe of frog,
> Wool of bat, and tongue of dog,
> Adder's fork, and blind-worm's sting,
> Lizard's leg, and howlet's wing,
> . . . .
> Scale of dragon, tooth of wolf,
> Witches' mummy, maw and gulf

Of the ravin'd salt-sea shark.
Root of hemlock digg'd i' the dark,
Liver of blaspheming Jew,
Gall of goat, and slips of yew
Sliver'd in the moon's eclipse,
Nose of Turk and Tartar's lips,
Finger of birth-strangled babe
Ditch-deliver'd by a drab,

. . . .

Cool it with a baboon's blood,
Then the charm is firm and good.

all this is not a figment of Shakespeare's vivid and bottomless imagination. It is taken from an actual black-magic incantation which he would certainly have known about during those years in which he lived in Stratford.

After a time gap of four centuries one can only speculate as to what was in Shakespeare's mind when he did this. Did he or did he not know just what he was doing? Did he, like many enlightened men, dismiss witchcraft and all that appertained to it as superstitious nonsense? Or did he have a healthy respect for it? We shall never know. But he was trespassing on forbidden ground. It is not safe to tamper with the forces of evil or use them for frivolous purposes. An appeal to the powers of darkness will not go unanswered. Nor did they in this case. For in using a real black-magic incantation, Shakespeare placed a curse on the play which has dogged it for four centuries.

The first performance of *Macbeth* took place in the evening of August 7, 1606, in the Great Hall at Hampton Court. Macbeth was played by Richard Burbage, the company's leading actor and a tragedian who enjoyed a very great popularity with the public on the strength of his performances as Hamlet, Richard III, King Lear, and Malvolio. His handsome, bearded face stares quizzically at posterity from his portrait and gives no indication that he was, alas, short and fat, but these physical handicaps were of little account beside the splendor of his voice, the nobility of his bearing, and the strength and dignity of his acting.

Separating facts from legend is difficult when writing about Shakespeare, for one is constantly brought up to face the sad realization that there are so few facts; but one has emerged. It seems that the curse did not waste any time before making its presence felt, for on this night of all nights, the boy actor who played Lady Macbeth, Hal Berridge, was suddenly taken ill with a fever, and at such short notice that the only possible substitute was the author himself. Since he had written the play and had directed the rehearsals, it could be hopefully assumed that he had more than a passing acquaintance with the text, and with its four brief scenes, Lady Macbeth is the shortest leading part he ever wrote.

The man we have to thank for this piece of vital information is that charming old gossip, John Aubrey. He was born ten years after Shakespeare died, but he loved the theatre and theatre people and knew a number of the King's Men in their old age and their sons. In his many writings he reported faithfully everything he heard from them, and whereas seventeenth-century gossip cannot be accepted completely, it should not be totally ignored.

One can only sympathize with Shakespeare and his company when confronted by this appalling crisis, and it needs no great effort of the imagination to visualize the panic and nervous distress that would have thus descended on them. Anyone who has been involved in a theatrical first performance knows how painful is the occasion. When it is a royal event, the tensions are considerably multiplied. One can easily see the hasty reallocation of parts, the hurried extra rehearsals in the Great Hall, the inevitable delay in starting, and the knife-edge tension on which the whole performance would have taken place. Theatrical tradition has suggested that there were other disasters that evening, but unfortunately tradition has not been specific. But a play performed in a dark gloomy hall lit only by candlelight which involves fire and blood, ghostly apparitions and realistic scenes of witchcraft, bloodstained fights, murders, and battles acted by a small team of tired, overworked, and under-rehearsed actors is bound to have its fair share of trouble.

Trouble, however, did come from another and unexpected source. Shakespeare's well-meaning attempts to please the king seem to have failed sadly, for there is evidence that James was not at all pleased with the play. Since Shakespeare was not one of the royal intimates, he would not have known about the king's squeamishness and allergy to the sight of cold steel. And here was a play with more deaths, stabbings, murders, fights, and battles than any he had written. And there was James, trapped in his seat as guest of honor, sitting in the front of the audience close to the action and forced to witness sights that were so unpleasant and distressing. Death and murders were portrayed in the Elizabethan theatre with a grossness and realism that we would now find disgusting. Blood and guts from the butcher's shop would be spilled over the stage in large quantities. The realism and authenticity of the witches' scenes would undoubtedly have upset him, and the murder of Duncan would have been an unfortunate reminder of the perils of his own life.

Royal disfavor had one immediate effect on the play—it was banned for five years. Between 1606 and 1611 there is no record anywhere of *Macbeth* being performed either in public or in private. The first known performance after the premiere was in 1611 in the Globe Theatre, and it was witnessed by the theatre-loving lawyer and astrologer, Simon Forman. The Hecate scenes had been added, there were music and dancing, and Macbeth and Banquo rode onto the stage on real horses. Forman's account is of great interest and value, as it is the first written account of a performance of the play. After that, *Macbeth* seems to have disappeared from the repertoire. The Globe was burned down shortly after and with it all the scenery, properties, costumes, and manuscripts that had kept the company going so long and so successfully.

Macbeth vanished from the theatre for nearly fifty years, for there are no records of any production until it appeared again in

1667, extensively rewritten by Sir William Davenant to suit the irredeemably trivial tastes of Restoration playgoers and barely recognizable as the play Shakespeare wrote. With music by Matthew Locke and songs, dances, and divertisements and what appears from contemporary accounts to have been a flying ballet, it emerged as a charming light opera which was seen and admired by that indefatigable theatregoer, Samuel Pepys:

> . . . to the Play-House where we saw MACBETH which is one of the best plays for stage and variety of dancing and musique that ever I saw. . . . (*Diary*, April 19, 1667)

Converting a tragedy into a musical seems to have had a slightly discouraging effect on the curse, for it appears that it went underground during the Restoration and there is little record of trouble during the last years of the seventeenth century. But at the turn of the eighteenth, a strange wave of puritanism swept through the land, and once again the theatre came under fire. Most active and voluble in this attack was the reformer, Jeremy Collier, who wrote a pamphlet *Dissuasive from the Play-House* (1703), in which he bitterly attacked those playwrights who used music "to disguise their obscene proplogues and unchaste wits" and thereby made their entertainments more attractive to the public than church services. The play that aroused his most bitter anger was *Macbeth*, for how could an interminable sermon on morality compete with Hecate and three Singing Witches at Covent Garden? In that year 1703, after a long absence from the stage, *Macbeth* was revived in its musical version, the management having characteristically defied the press, the Deity, and augury in order to provide the public with what it confidently described as a wholesome and enriching entertainment. The moralists gloomily and gloatingly prophesied disaster, and for once they were right. While *Macbeth* was still playing, the worst storm in England's history occurred: fifteen hundred seamen were killed, a million pounds of damage was done in London, and the city of Bristol was totally destroyed. The moralists were triumphant, and Jeremy Collier announced that the hurricane was an expression of God's anger at a playwright who "mocke'd the great governour of the World who alone commands the wind and the seas." Queen Anne declared a day of fasting and humiliation to appease God, and the theatres closed down for a full week. Davenant's musical-comedy trimmings are another example of the extraordinary bad luck that has dogged *Macbeth*. More than any other Shakespeare play, *Macbeth* has suffered at the hands of hack writers who believed that they could improve on the original and that the play must, on all accounts, be rewritten. After Davenant, it was David Garrick who improved it and attempted thereby to restore the play to its tragic stature. His famous revival of 1744 placed him firmly in the front rank of popular tragedians. He cut out many of Davenant's improvements and being a frustrated playwright he could not forbear to write in that very death scene that Shakespeare had taken so much trouble to avoid, producing in the process some of the most ludicrously inept blank verse in the history of the theatre.

Tis done! The scene of my life will quickly close!
Ambitions vain delusive dreams are fled
And now I wake in darkness and guilt.
I cannot bear it, let me shake it off.
It will not be, my soul is clogged with blood.
I cannot rise! I dare not ask for mercy.
It is too late; hell drags me down.
     I sink.
I sink, I sink, my soul is fled for ever . . . Oh! Oh!

An actress who, although it gave her the greatest success of her career, was to believe firmly in the intrinsic evil of the play and for whom it was a nightly ordeal to appear in it, was Mrs. Siddons. She was a young and inexperienced actress of twenty-one when she first played in it, touring in the west of England in the winter of 1775. Owing to a sudden illness in the company, she was told only the night before that she was to play Lady Mac-

Mrs. Siddons in a later Macbeth

beth. She had never played the part before and there were to be no rehearsals. Horrifying as this may sound to contemporary theatre people, it was taken for granted that in the popular classics the company knew their allotted parts and that further rehearsals would not be necessary. It was an old custom and beginners had to sink or swim. Mrs. Siddons took the play to her room and prepared to stay up all night, learning it by candlelight. "I went on with tolerable composure in the silence of the night," she later wrote in her memoirs, "till I came to the assassination scene. The horrors of the scene rose to such a degree that made it impossible to get further. I snatched up a candle and hurried out the room in a paroxysm of terror. My dress was of silk and the rustling of it, as I ascended the stairs to go to bed, seemed to my panic-stricken fancy like the movements of a spectre pursuing me. I capt my candlestick and threw myself on my bed where I lay without daring even to take my clothes off."

The following night she played Lady Macbeth for the first time and gave what she admitted to be the worst performance of her career. The evil generated by the play still gripped her, and she was pale, nervous, and ineffectual. She did not know the lines and the number of prompts she received was phenomenal. The audience showed its displeasure in the customary rowdy eighteenth-century provincial manner, and her embarrassment and mortification were complete. Never, she vowed, would she play Lady Macbeth again with inadequate rehearsal.

The full text of the play as Shakespeare wrote it was not restored to the public until Kemble revived it in 1794 at Drury Lane with Mrs. Siddons, his sister, and with the text came back the curse. Throughout the nineteenth and twentieth centuries *Macbeth* has had a very turbulent history of accidents. Cynics will point out that if the play is disaster prone, then there are sensible reasons for this. They will state that the play is immensely popular with actors and audiences and, with the possible exception of *Hamlet*, is revived more than any other Shakespeare play, that the twenty-six short scenes which make up Shakespeare's shortest play mean quick lighting and furniture changes. They state that most of the play takes place at night, which means dim lighting and sometimes total darkness; that there are more duels, fights, murders, and battles than in any other Shakespeare play. These disbelievers will triumphantly say: if you have up to thirty actors wearing the heavy and traditionally awkward costumes and armor used for the play rushing up and down the stairs, rostrums, and bridges of the inevitable permanent set and in the dark, then by the simple law of averages there are bound to be a number of accidents. This is indisputably true. But when all this has been said, when the curse has been dismissed as superstitious nonsense and the disasters as so many coincidences, when it has been firmly pointed out that if you believe in the bad luck then it will come, you are still left with an appalling amount of trouble which simply cannot be explained away.

Four hundred years of death, doom, and disaster offer an intimidatingly large field of investigation. During the seventeenth and eighteenth centuries the information, coming largely from the occasional memoir and diary, is naturally a little sparse. During the nineteenth century, with the arrival of the popular press, the documentation is noticeably better; but with the present century and with so many of the actors involved still happily alive to describe their experiences with the play, it is possible to recount them with a wealth of colorful (if contradictory) detail. Where does one start, for there is an *embarras de richnesse?* But a random choice from the last fifty years has produced some deeply interesting and disturbing case histories.

A typical one is the famous 1937 revival at the Old Vic with the thirty-year-old Laurence Olivier playing the part for the first time, following his sensational triumph in the complete *Hamlet* at the beginning of the year. The director was Michel St. Denis who had enjoyed a distinguished and controversial career in Paris with the avant-garde theatre and had recently settled in London. He had started a drama school and had directed John Gielgud in André Obey's *Noah.* This revival of *Macbeth* was his first Shakespeare play. The invitation had been extended to him at the insistence of Tyrone Guthrie who not only had a heavy production schedule himself but was anxious to bring in new ideas and new blood to the Old Vic and rescue it from the dusty insularity which had inspired one wit to describe the theatre as "La Tragedie Anglaise." The invitation had been fiercely opposed by Lilian Baylis, the matriarchal founder and director of the Old Vic, who disliked and distrusted foreigners and feared the evil influence they might possibly have on *her* actors and *her* theatre (her love was both jealous and possessive).

It became speedily obvious that what seemed an excellent idea in theory wasn't going to work out in practice. The great difficulty was the unforeseen language barrier. Michel St. Denis spoke a little fractured English and few of the company spoke enough French. The chief sufferer in this was his Macbeth. Olivier was tackling for the first time what is arguably Shakespeare's most difficult part, and he urgently needed help, advice, and encouragement. The director's spirit was certainly willing but the language was weak. Long discussions in garbled English, torrential French, and mime on the inner meaning of the play, the historical background, and the deeper motivation of the part were no substitute for hard theatrical instruction. The ideas seemed to be original when St. Denis could be understood, but throughout the company there was a nagging suspicion that the French had never really liked or understood Shakespeare, and that St. Denis was concerned only with the play's visual possibilities rather than its true theatrical meaning. Michel St. Denis was that most tiresome of all theatrical birds, the experimental perfectionist with a dozen different meanings and subtleties for every line, but very little practicality.

The production was immensely complicated and made extensive use of masks, weird symbolic lighting, multiple scene changes, and all the outward manifestations of continental expressionism. The production might have succeeded if St. Denis had three months to rehearse and an unlimited budget, but in those tightly scheduled Old Vic seasons, rehearsals were for only three weeks and there was very little money. The company was virtually self-supporting, and the budget was pitifully small, top salary being £10 weekly.

The company was nervous and unhappy and the troubles started without delay. St. Denis and his friend, Vera Lindsey, who played Lady Macduff, were traveling back from a party when the taxi braked suddenly to avoid a collision. They were thrown violently forward and crashed their heads against the glass partition which resulted in some very nasty bruises and cuts. The next day when they appeared at the theatre, bandaged and stitched and pale, one of the company sighed deeply and said for all to hear, "Oh, dear, the bad luck has started already." Michel St. Denis did not understand the remark and it had to be explained that *Macbeth* has a history of bad luck. He shrugged his shoulders, but there was a distinct feeling in the company that he was seriously worried, not only by the curse but the probable effect it would have on the company morale. Company morale deteriorated still further the next day when Lilian Baylis's little dog was killed by a passing motorcar. She had lavished all her accumulated affection on the animal, and its death affected her very deeply.

By the end of the third week the production was under-rehearsed and far from ready: it was quite obvious that it could not possibly open in time. The first night was on Tuesday, but when the dress rehearsal started on the Sunday before, it was discovered to everybody's horror that the elaborate sets did not fit. They were too big, so they had to be taken back to the workshops and cut down to size. Then the accumulated effects of overwork and nervous strain took their further toll on Olivier, who developed a bad cold and finally lost his voice completely and could speak only in a whisper. Postponement till Friday was inevitable, a drastic decision, for the plays followed every four weeks in those tightly scheduled prewar Old Vic seasons. There were hundreds of loyal patrons who had regular bookings for every play. Lilian Baylis had never had to do it before, she hated to disappoint her public, and she took it very badly. Since it was clear that St. Denis could not cope, Tyrone Guthrie was called in by Lilian Baylis to take over the production, to pull it together, and get it on the stage within three days. This he proceeded to do and with characteristic generosity refused to take a credit in the program or to allow the news to be leaked to the press. During these four days the company were worked morning, evening, and night. Morale was naturally low and it sunk still lower when Olivier was nearly killed. He was sitting in the wings talking to Vera Lindsey. He was called and rose to go onto the stage. Shortly after he left his seat, a stage weight weighing twenty-five pounds crashed down on to the seat from the flies, crushing it to fragments. He had missed death by seconds.

But worse was to come. Lilian Baylis had to go home early on the Wednesday, and it was reported to the company that she was seriously ill. Everybody prayed for her recovery, prayed that these dreadful rehearsal weeks would conclude without further trouble, but it was not to be. When the company came to the theatre on Friday for the final dress rehearsal, they were greeted with the news they had all been dreading—Lilian Baylis had died of a heart attack in her home. She was sixty-five. It was the end of an era. Never again would that fat, myopic figure in the red doctorate robes be seen in the stage box. For the company, Friday night's first performance was an unforgettably sad, traumatic evening, sustained only by the knowledge that her last message had been an anxious inquiry that everything was all right at the Vic and her desire that the show should go on. They played together magnificently, and Olivier gave what he later considered the most passionate and emotional performance of his life. When he finally returned to his dressing room, he found a note from Lilian Baylis which her secretary had thoughtfully withheld until the end of the performance. "Welcome return to dear Laurence Olivier. May you be as happy in Macbeth as in Hamlet last season."

The notices were excellent and the press played up the curse of

Macbeth relentlessly in the popular papers throughout the four-week run. The public, loving the play and intrigued by the melodramatic sensationalism of the whole matter, flocked to Waterloo Road and filled the house night after night. It was certainly this factor that prompted Bronson Albery to transfer the production to the New Theatre for a three-week season before Christmas. It was a disaster. The pre-Christmas month is traditionally a bad time for the theatre and the West End public (very different then from the Old Vic public) was not interested in an avant-garde, cheaply mounted *Macbeth* without big West End star names, and the production played to dispiritingly empty houses.

And so it ended not with a bang but a whimper, but even the saddest whimper can produce one amusing incident. Such a one did occur and thus provided Olivier with one of his favorite stories which he tells against himself and has generously allowed to be included in this book. One afternoon the matinee audience was exceptionally sparse, with acres of empty stalls, but in the stage box sat a young schoolboy who was watching the play with keen, intelligent eyes. Olivier found this very encouraging; he acted up and directed his entire performance to the boy in the box. The rest of the company did likewise and never had a performance of *Macbeth* been thundered, screamed, and howled with such intensity as was this to its youthful and appreciative audience of one. During the interval, Olivier remarked to John Merivale, his Macduff, with a touch of complacency, "That boy will never see anything like this as long as he lives; it's an experience he'll never forget." But when they all returned to the stage after the interval, the boy had gone.

In 1955 Olivier played his second Macbeth at Stratford with Vivien Leigh as his Lady and Keith Michell as Macduff in a production by Glen Byham Shaw. This was one of the few cases where the curse was known to have taken a holiday, for apart from a couple of little accidents in the duel scene (Olivier nicked the white of Keith Michell's eye during rehearsals, and himself

nearly fell twenty feet from a high rostrum in one of the early performances), rehearsals and performances took place without
much incident. Olivier scored one of his greatest successes in this
part, and those few who were lucky enough to have seen it are
agreed that it is indisputably the finest Macbeth our generation
has seen. Keith Michell was a very dashing, passionate Macduff,
and Vivien Leigh brought an unsuspected vocal depth and dignity and dramatic tension to the Lady. Shaw's production was
sensible, atmospheric, full of imagination, and was in every respect a triumph for all concerned. A film version had been in
Olivier's mind for some years and now was the time. It seemed
the most natural thing in the world that he should thus complete
the quartet begun with the immensely popular, prestigious, and
money-spinning *Henry V*, *Hamlet*, and *Richard III*. Backers were
found, a script was prepared, Olivier grew a beard, and a little
preliminary casting was done round the Oliviers as the Macbeths.
Then disaster struck: the backers backed out and the money was
not forthcoming. J. Arthur Rank wasn't interested, and the major
American distributors decided that Olivier was not box office.
This smear had been pursuing him for some years, and it was one
of those maddening half-truths which it was difficult to deny in
toto. Admittedly his last two films, *Carrie* and *The Beggar's Opera*
had not been successful; in fact the latter had been a total disaster.
But his three Shakespeare films had all made a profit over a period
of years. This was not enough for the moguls of Wardour Street:
they wanted large profits instantly. If Korda had been alive there
would have been no problem, but Korda was dead. Olivier traveled round, hopefully looking for the money until two days
before shooting was due to start in Scotland, before finally ad-
mitting defeat. The film was put up on the shelf and has never
been taken down. This story, typical of the appalling and sheer
wanton stupidity of the film world, is enough to make any theatre
person weep. Thanks to all those faceless, nameless film moguls,
our greatest actor's greatest performance has been allowed to
become a slowly blurring memory. Posterity's loss is in-

cellent. It was clearly going to be the most exciting production any of them had ever been in.

A few days later the troubles started. A local man, employed in the theatre offices, collapsed in the theatre's assembly hall one day and died in the hospital of a heart attack. It was an indication of Peter Hall's success with his morale-building talk that this was not regarded as a sinister omen. But a few days after that, Peter Hall himself collapsed and was taken to the hospital with shingles, a particularly nasty and painful affliction. He had for some time been fighting a running battle with bad health and nervous fatigue. Three years earlier he had had a nervous breakdown, and this second onslaught was evidence that he had not properly recovered. For six weeks he had to lie on his back in a dark and silent room. It was rumored that he would go blind, but this turned out to be, happily, a false alarm. In his absence the governors had to make a decision—to postpone or not to postpone. Since there was nobody else to take over the production, and since Peter Hall himself was very anxious to see it to a successful conclusion, it was decided that a postponement was inevitable. Tickets were refunded, the entire autumn schedule was revised, and many thousands of overseas visitors were disappointed. In his absence the production was placed in cold storage. From time to time they would do a run-through under Paul Scofield's supervision, but clearly little extra could be contributed.

Peter Hall returned in late July and was photographed outside the theatre smiling happily with Paul Scofield and Vivien Merchant. All seemed to be satisfactory, but it was not so. He tried to galvanize the company into their former enthusiasm, but it was not possible. The excitement and the fun had gone, and it became speedily evident that he was still not well. His physical energy, his enthusiasm, and the flow of ideas had gone. The company morale sank very low. It went even lower when the costumes arrived. They looked magnificent but they were made of plastic which was very heavy and hot. The final rehearsals and the opening performances took place in the middle of August during a heat wave, and to this day the company remembers the torture of those evenings, sweating away in the punishing heat of the theatre. In fact, it was only the regular supply of salt tablets that enabled them to get through a performance.

The notices were mixed though respectful. Audiences were on the whole very enthusiastic and the play did capacity business for the rest of the season, but the feeling of disappointment throughout the company was keen. American television wanted to film it and contracts were in preparation, but it was eventually decided to cancel it. "The production just didn't work," Peter Hall wrote to me years later. "It didn't recover from its postponement and I, being ill, stuck rigidly to my original conception instead of modifying it. In the circumstances it seemed better not to film it. BUT I MEAN TO DO THE PLAY AGAIN."

Another man who is determined to direct *Macbeth* again is Anthony Tuckey, of the Liverpool Repertory Theatre. The first time was in early 1970, and the sequence of disasters was so extraordinary that a chill goes through the whole of the theatre whenever the production is mentioned. Before he started rehearsals he talked to a number of other prominent repertory managers who had previously directed the play. All, without exception, advised him to abandon the idea. He refused to take their advice. The troubles began in the second week. John Franklyn Robbins, playing Macbeth, was hit in the eye by a sword and the membrane covering the eye was scratched, an accident, not very serious, but it did involve a complete rest. On the same day, Barbara Ewing, playing Lady Macbeth, went down with flu. Anthony Tuckey took over Macbeth and Audrey Barr, one of the witches, deputized for the Lady. This left a gap in the witches' scenes and an actress, Liz Gebhardt, visiting her husband in Liverpool, found herself at an hour's notice striking her head through a trap door and choking to death in the smoke while she quavered one of the vision's lines. The flu spread, and by the end of the second week there were five understudies playing. An urgent message was sent to Jack Lynn, who had just played the part at Chesterfield, but as he was still suffering from severe head injuries sustained during his opening-night final duel, he declined.

By the end of the third week the company was together again and in good health. After a rehearsal on Saturday, Tuckey wished them good luck for the last performance and said how glad he was that they had survived their troubles. Unbelievably, he spoke too soon. Bob Harris, the actor who was playing the Bloody Sergeant, went out for a stroll at about 7 P.M. and carefully adjusted his watch by a public clock. He had not been long in Liverpool or he would have known that this particular clock has always stood at thirteen minutes past six. He thus confidently extended his walk and eventually returned to the theatre to be greeted with the horror-stricken news that the play had started twenty minutes earlier and that he had missed his scene. The supreme irony is that the play got the best notices for years and played to full houses.

There are many who do not believe in this ancient superstition, and do not believe in *any* superstition. The concept of bad luck does not exist for them. Many of these are sufficiently sensible and diplomatic to keep their private thoughts on the subject to themselves; many are not. The powers of evil do not require that every actor should believe in them, but they do get very angry and aggressive if they are laughed at and made the target for mockery. It is necessary to respect them, and it is even more necessary to respect your colleagues, particularly those with whom you share a dressing room. A young actor might quote from *Macbeth* accidentally, which is very easy to do. He will inevitably be taken to task by some older actor, gently or not so gently. What he must do is to perform a simple ritual or exorcism which is traditionally thus: to go out of the dressing room, turn around three times, spit, knock on the door three times, and beg humbly for readmission. The alternative is to quote a famous line from *The Merchant of Venice*, "Fair thoughts and happy hours attend on you." *The Merchant* is a lucky play, and its text has a traditional exorcising effect on *Macbeth*. What the young actor must definitely *not* do is to laugh contemptuously and say that he doesn't believe in any of that superstitious nonsense and to continue quoting the play in defiance of all decency or common sense. The story of *Macbeth* is full of tragic incidents where young actors (and some not so young, too) have deliberately defied augury and even insulted it with disastrous consequences.

Diana Wynyard played Lady Macbeth at Stratford in 1948 with Sir Godfrey Tearle's Macbeth and directed by Michael Benthall. She didn't believe in the curse and made the sad mistake of saying so shortly after the dress rehearsal. Just before she went on for the sleep-walking scene, she decided that the way she had been rehearsing it, and the traditional way of playing it, was all wrong. Sleepwalkers did *not* walk with their eyes open, as they had always been shown. They walked with their eyes *shut*, and without telling anybody she went on the stage on the first night and put the theory into practice. The rostrum was wide enough for comfort, and, as she had been rehearsing it for several days, she thought she knew exactly how far it went and at what point it started to curve round. The first-night audience gasped audibly with horror as she slipped from the rostrum and fell fifteen feet. It was a mark of her professionalism that she picked herself up and continued with the scene, and of her courage that, although bruised, bandaged, and considerably shaken, she did not miss any performances.

An actress in the cast of *Irma La Douce* was foolish enough to quote from *Macbeth* in the wings while waiting to go on, and carried the folly still further by refusing to take seriously the concern of the actors in the wings. That evening the car in which she was being driven home crashed, and although neither she nor the driver was seriously hurt, she was badly shaken. Two days later she went down with food poisoning and had to miss a number of performances. Martin Jarvis, playing Hamlet at Windsor, in 1973, remembers the evening in which an old colleague started to quote from the play at great length just before his appearance. An hour later he suffered an agonizing lapse of memory, and a long speech, which had previously given him no trouble whatever, suddenly vanished from his mind and resulted in a lively duet with the prompter. That same performance, Polonius suffered a stroke and had to retire from the company. The fact that my letter, asking if he had had any *Macbeth* experiences, arrived at the theatre on that very evening was just a sinister coincidence. Actors at the Old Vic remember a young actor who quoted from *Macbeth* during a performance of *The Merchant of Venice*, in the middle fifties. The sad, predictable pattern followed. The actors told him not to, he laughed contemptuously, and refused to believe what he described as nonsense. Within a few minutes three actors suffered physical injuries in connection with a rather lethal piece of mobile scenery—broken toes, broken fingers, and bruised shins. After the performance, the young actor stepped out of the stage door and was promptly knocked over by a car. He wasn't hurt, only bruised and shaken, but he did then admit that there might be something in all the nonsense, and from that time on he was careful never to quote the play again.

The staff of London's New Theatre during the run of *Oliver* remember with horror the night a young girl, employed as a temporary usherette, was waiting in the front lobby for the show to finish and whiled away the time by quoting *Macbeth*, "tomorrow and tomorrow and tomorrow . . ." She was severely reprimanded by a senior member of the staff, a cloakroom attendant. The young girl was, it seems, suitably apologetic, but it was too late. A few minutes later one of the actors, Claude Jones, rushing across the bridge in the final scene, fell to the stage, fractured his skull, and died instantly.

Mocking Shakespeare in musicals and revues is frowned on and never seems to be very successful, but mocking *Macbeth* is really dangerous. It was Charles Cochran who decided to include a Herbert Farjeon sketch about *Macbeth* in his wartime (1942) revue, *Big Top*. He wasn't superstitious at all even though the sketch involved extensive quotation and misquotation from the text of the play; it was called "Mockbeth." Beatrice Lillie was the star, and in this sketch she did indescribably funny things with her kilt, sporran, bagpipes, and the inevitable rope of pearls. A few old actors were heard to mutter nervously, but the hysterical laughter she drew from the wartime audience seemed justification enough.

> Where shall we three meet again?
> The Vic, the New or Drury Lane?
> What hags are those with their soup tureen?
> The middle one looks more like Basil Dean!

But a double tragedy was to follow. Within one week, shortly after the show opened, an actor in the company, whose name really was Robin Hood, lost his father, and Beatrice Lillie received the tragic news that her only son, then serving in the Royal Navy, had been killed in action. He was a tall, handsome boy, the apple of her eye, and her bereavement and the effect it had on her are most movingly described in her autobiography.

Nicholas Hawtrey, an actor from Stratford, had always viewed the superstition with disbelief. His mother had at one time been the curator of the Ellen Terry house in Smallhythe which was also used as a theatre museum, and among the exhibits was Ellen Terry's famous and magnificent Lady Macbeth costume which had been designed (and later painted in a portrait) by Whistler. Hawtrey was there one day when it was being moved while the house was to be spring-cleaned. A small jewel fell off from the crown, and he retrieved it, deciding to adopt it as a lucky mascot. A diamond from Ellen Terry's *Macbeth* costume would certainly carry some status.

For some years he cherished it, but it brought nothing but bad luck and so much of it that he finally decided to return it to the Ellen Terry museum. He was still not entirely convinced, so he put the superstition to a further test during the 1959 season at Stratford. Every night for a period of several weeks he quoted from *Macbeth* in his dressing room and persuaded the other actors to do likewise, just to see what happened. His curiosity was

Sincerely,
Beatrice Lillie

*Beatrice Lillie, who appeared in a revue sketch, "Mockbeth,"
with tragic results*

quickly satisfied. There was a succession of small troubles, nothing very serious, but enough to make one wonder. Actors suffered strange lapses of memory, fell backward off high rostrums, injured themselves in fights. There were small technical troubles, light bulbs failing at crucial moments and sound equipment fusing during vital scene changes. There were administrative troubles. Paul Robeson announced that he would not after all be appearing as Othello and a replacement had to be found. Every time the play was quoted, Nicholas Hawtrey remembers, something bad happened. Finally he was convinced, and to everybody's relief the experiment was abandoned.

A similar experiment was tried by the actors in *Antony and Cleopatra* at the Bankside Theatre in the summer of 1973. Several of them in a dressing room started to shout out a speech from *Macbeth* just to see what would happen. The immediate result was a scene from a Hammer horror film. A storm blew up, a truly terrible storm which produced a savage deluge of rain. This beat down on the canvas roof which began to sag and fill up. In the meantime, the electricity from the storm caused a very dangerous short-circuiting, and the whole stage became an electric death trap. The performance was thankfully stopped, the audience sent away, the roof collapsed, and the theatre virtually fell to pieces. Such extensive repairs were required that the 1974 season had to be canceled.

The most appalling incident in this category was always known in the profession as The Oldham Tragedy. Some of those involved have suffered such a deep shock that even after almost thirty years they will not talk about it. The Oldham Repertory Company decided to celebrate its ninth anniversary with a production of *Macbeth*. The part was to be played by their leading man, Harold Norman, who was popular in the town and with the company. He was a very talented actor and had recently played Iago, Ernest, and Mr. Rochester. A great future was prophesied for him; he was at this time thirty-four. He was married to a young dancer, Audrey Kaye, and they had a baby daughter. The company included Bernard Cribbins (Seyton), Weyman Mackay (Malcolm), Harry Lomax (Duncan), and Antony Oakley (Macduff). It was directed by Douglas Emery. Norman and Oakley were given instructions to rehearse their fight, with sword and dagger, alone and on their own time, which they did with enormous enthusiasm and professional expertise. Both daggers and swords were blunted as is the theatrical custom. The play opened on Monday, January 27, 1947. It went very well, Norman gave a fine performance, and the company received good notices. On Wednesday night, January 30, Douglas Emery was standing in the wings watching the fight that ends the play between Macbeth and Macduff. Both actors were stabbing and hacking with their usual energy, but it did seem that the moves were slightly muddled and weren't running as strictly as they should according to the rehearsed routine. This night it was cut short, for Norman fell to the ground, but instead of dying on stage as it had been rehearsed, he crawled slowly to the wings. "Douglas, I've been stabbed, I can't take my curtain call," he whispered. Emery sent for an ambulance and Norman was taken off to the local hospital. In the meantime the play had finished and the audience was shouting for Norman who had given a magnificent performance. Douglas Emery then had to go in front of the curtain and explain what had happened to a hushed and shocked audience. The following afternoon the senior surgical officer at the hospital decided that there was evidence of bowel perforation and performed an operation. Norman made what appeared to be a good recovery. The Oldham *Chronicle* decided not to swamp a trivial incident with a lot of sensational publicity about the superstition and said very little about it. The part of Macbeth was played in Harold Norman's absence by the stage manager, Arthur Hall. But a few weeks later general peritonitis set in and exactly a month after the stabbing, Norman died.

At the inquest, evidence was given by the stage staff, the other actors, the medical authorities, and the firm that hires out theatre daggers. Antony Oakley stated that he had never met Norman before they joined the company and that their professional relationship had always been very friendly. He was completely exonerated and the official verdict was death by misadventure. But a little later it was reported that Norman's baby had died of suffocation, and his widow had suffered a nervous breakdown as a result of the double tragedy and had left the theatre. It was a quarter of a century after the tragedy that it was learned that, a little time before the production, Norman had shared a dressing room with an older actor and had started to quote *Macbeth*. He disdainfully ignored the tearful requests that he should stop because it was bad luck and continued to quote. Six weeks later he was dead.

Two people who did believe in the curse most religiously and who never scoffed at it were Sybil Thorndike and Lewis Casson. In 1926 they presented the play at the Prince's Theatre (now the Shaftesbury), with Henry Ainley as Macbeth, Sybil and Lewis as Lady Macbeth and Banquo, Basil Gill as Macduff, and the youthful Jack Hawkins as Fleance. They invested a lot of their own money in it, which has long been regarded as very bad luck. From the start it was one of those productions that goes wrong in every department. Lewis, who directed, was at his snappiest and angriest during rehearsals, and he and Sybil bickered and quarreled more violently than ever before. Bernard Shaw came to the rehearsals and tried to take over the production, making a fool of himself with his stupid comments and instructions (his directorial skills did not, it seemed, extend to other people's plays); at one point, as Jack Hawkins remembered, he had a blazing screaming match with John Laurie over the correct pronunciation of Scone, which Shaw insisted should be said *skoon* to rhyme with moon. The first performance went well and the notices were good, but a series of mysterious troubles hit the theatre like the plague. Costumes caught fire, scenery fell down, and equipment was stolen.

To cap it all, Henry Ainley, suffering from nervous exhaustion and fighting his lifelong battle with alcoholism, had to leave the company. His place was taken by Hubert Carter, a huge, bull-necked, bull-voiced heavyweight actor who had so little control over his natural strength that he nearly killed Sybil on one occasion and nearly killed his Macduff on several successive nights. The company became very worried and tense, and there were nights when Sybil was frightened to go onto the stage and had to force herself by a real effort of will.

One evening, Lewis took her into their dressing room: "Sybil, the Devil *does* work in this play," he said; "there *is* horror behind it. The play is truly cursed." Together they knelt down and prayed, reciting the 91st Psalm, "surely he shall deliver us from this noisome pestilence." Slowly the aura of evil and darkness lifted, they went on the stage without any further fears, and the remainder of its regrettably short run passed without incident.

Quotation can be dangerous even outside a theatre if the context is nevertheless a theatrical one. Noel Johnson remembers an ENSA tour in the war of *Thunder Rock*. The company traveled from one theatre to the next in a coach. One evening during the journey, one of the company started to quote from *Macbeth* and stopped in midsentence as the others exploded with vituperation. It was then democratically decided that the mischief had been done and that they might just as well continue quoting. So, like naughty children working off years of repression doing what was forbidden, the entire company started to quote their favourite passages from *Macbeth*. That night, the performance of *Thunder Rock* was one long accident. Nothing very serious happened, but a succession of little troubles reduced the play to something resembling chaos. Props were mislaid, scenery fell over, costumes were torn, entrances were missed, lines were forgotten, and in a fight between Noel Johnson and Humphrey Morton, the latter was knocked momentarily unconscious by a mistimed blow. In the journey back, the company was wryly discussing the evening's disasters. Suddenly somebody remembered the journey to the theatre earlier that evening. "My God," he said, "do you remember what play we were all quoting?"

Clayre Ribner, general manager of the Shakespeare Festival at Stratford, Connecticut, remembers a truly terrible season in 1961. The company included Pat Hingle, Jessica Tandy, Kim Hunter, and Will Geer. The first accident occurred during the dress rehearsal of *Macbeth*. One of the company riding a bicycle to the theatre was knocked over by a car and had to spend a week in the hospital. During a preview performance, the stage lift taking up the three witches rose too high, one of the witches stepped forward onto the darkened stage, fell, and injured herself badly. She had to spend some days in the hospital. Throughout the summer they were plagued with injuries and accidents, and the local doctor was in constant attendance.

Franklin Cover replaced Pat Hingle as Macbeth for the final month of the season and had to play the dagger scene at a command performance at the White House in front of President John F. Kennedy and Sudan's General Ibrahin, the first time Shakespeare had ever been performed there.

He had a very painful time with the play. One night he was chasing a witch in Act One and took a fall, landing on his back and missing a fog machine by inches. He lay there painfully for what seemed like hours until Banquo's solicitous, "My gracious Lord, may I help you?" brought down the house in mocking laughter. X rays were taken, and, although nothing had been broken, he was black and blue for days. Later he developed a cyst under his left arm. It was operated on and he played the remaining performances in great pain with blood soaking through the bandages. Complications developed when the dye of his costume worked its way inside, necessitating a further operation in New York. After all this, he firmly believes in the curse but, as with so many actors, would dearly love to risk it all again.

The climactic disaster of the season took place during this final month. Douglas Sherman, a young actor from the company, was found dying of knife wounds in the picnic grounds adjacent to the theatre. Police questioned everybody after the performance, but the murderer was not discovered. The following week, the little daughter of the actor Colgate Salsbury fell to her death from the window of the apartment they occupied. But still the curse was not satisfied, for Jack Landau, the company manager, was later murdered in his Boston apartment. Two young thugs were charged and subsequently released for lack of evidence.

In Minneapolis, a talented young actor, George Ostroska, playing his first Macbeth, collapsed and died of a heart attack while on the stage. By a strange irony, he was talking to the two murderers in the banquet scene, and had just come to the lines:

> There's blood on the face,
> Thou art the best of cut-throats.

In 1941, Margaret Webster directed the play with Maurice Evans and Judith Anderson. The preliminaries of casting were unusually acrimonious and produced one ferocious row between Margaret Webster and Maurice Evans. The rehearsals were reasonably smooth, but the physical production was immensely complicated. It involved light projections, which Margaret Webster had always disliked and distrusted, complex scene changes, recorded sound effects, a musical score in the pit, transparencies, and all the usual hazards, including Banquo's ghost, the witches, and the apparitions. No expense or trouble was to be stinted.

During the New Haven rehearsals, the stage manager got stage manager's stage fright, and became paralytic and helpless. The electrician caught the infection. The designer decided that his light projections were the most important aspect of the production and Margaret Webster decided that they were not. She finally had to tell him to leave the theatre and not come back till after the opening night.

The opening night in Boston was a real director's nightmare. None of the effects happened as they were intended and the performance was a mess. But this was nothing in comparison to the New York opening. All went well until the England scene in Act Four. When the lights came up, it proved to be Duncan's tent scene from Act One. The unhappy designer crept up to Margaret Webster in the darkness and whispered, "Another surprise for me?" She nodded sympathetically. "And for me, too," she said. It was only the rapid intervention of the stage manager who rushed up the iron ladder to the fly floor which stopped the overeager flymen from visibly changing the set when they discovered their mistake.

Immediately after the New York opening, Margaret Webster had appendicitis. Then Pearl Harbor happened and the draft began to bear down on the company; the thanes of Scotland and the lords of England began to disappear almost weekly. At the end of the New York run, a long road tour was planned, which involved some recasting, including Judith Anderson's understudy. Margaret Webster came down with flu at this point and could do little about it. The tour was to open at Buffalo on a Monday night in February and on Monday morning, Maurice Evans telephoned her to say that Judith Anderson had laryngitis and the new understudy did not yet know the lines. He suggested that she come up and play Lady Macbeth. She crawled out of bed and went to the airport. The flight was made very bumpy and dangerous by a blizzard which was in progress. Margaret Webster had played the part before and did know the lines, but she was not at all sure about the directorial moves and business she had devised, and throughout the flight she was continually closing her eyes and trying hard to remember them. To add to her troubles, she felt weak and ill. At last, a man sitting across the aisle spoke to her sympathetically. "I have some airsickness tablets, if you would like one," he said. She shook her head. "They're no good for what's troubling me." she said.

Happily she was able to get through the evening performance without disaster, and even with some credit. The next day at her hotel a huge and magnificent bouquet of flowers arrived with a card saying, "Never again will I mistake a rehearsal of the sleepwalking scene for airsickness." There was, however, a brief postscript to all this. Her production of *Macbeth* was selected at the end of the tour to be tried out at Fort Meade to demonstrate

whether the U.S. Army would like, or more probably loathe, Shakespeare. As she was on her way to join the company, acute tonsillitis set in and she had to return quickly to New York.

There was a bitter little epilogue to all this: the curse can produce many different sorts of trouble quite apart from the more obvious physical and artistic disasters—it can, indeed, be devious, patient, and malevolent. It had not quite finished with the Evans–Webster–Anderson production and chose a singularly unpleasant and long-delayed method to make its further presence felt—like a time bomb with a very long fuse, in this case twenty-six years, although the solitary victim was not anybody in or even remotely connected with the play.

Among those who saw it in its initial New York run was William Redfield, a boy actor of thirteen who had scored a great success in Moss Hart's production of *Junior Miss* and was to make a small but ineradicable mark on theatrical history by being the only actor to get star billing as Guildenstern which he played in the famous Burton *Hamlet*. After Redfield had seen the performance of *Macbeth*, he went backstage to visit a friend in the company who played Banquo. Sitting in Banquo's dressing room, they chatted and laughed, and Banquo told him a very funny and very well-known story about the English director, Basil Dean, and a difference of opinion he had had with Sir Ralph Richardson over a play in which they had both been involved back in the early thirties. Sixteen years later, Redfield published a brilliantly witty and vivid account of the rehearsals and performances of the Burton *Hamlet*. It was called *Letters to an Actor,* and it was plentifully garnished with amusing anecdotes. One of them was the Dean–Richardson story. It was published in England and Basil Dean, taking strong exception to the story, sued the English publisher. The vital point at issue was simple. Could Redfield prove that the story was true? Clearly, he couldn't, even though the story had been told and retold on both sides of the Atlantic for many years and was part of contemporary theatrical folklore. The suit was surrendered and there were no damages other than court costs, but the book was embargoed within two weeks of its En-

glish publication and both the publisher and William Redfield ended up by being considerably out of pocket.

Another actor who will always remember *Macbeth* with alarm and embarrassment is Charlton Heston. He had played it a number of times, including a very successful performance on NBC television, before he played it under Burgess Meredith's direction in an open-air production at Fort St. Catherine, Bermuda, in 1953. Trouble began at the rehearsals when Heston had a severe accident on his motorcycle. His legs were badly cut and he had to leave the company for a few days, which upset him very much, as never before in his life had he ever missed a single day's rehearsal. This was the point when other actors in the company began to talk about the curse and to quote examples of it from recent theatre history.

They did not have to wait long to see its effect, for trouble started right at the first performance. Jack Fletcher, who played the Porter, was sitting in the wings, watching Macbeth's first scene with Banquo. Heston left the stage abruptly and rushed to Fletcher, pointing at his tights. "Get them off me, get them off me," he whispered frantically. Fletcher and another actor grabbed him by the waist and pulled his tights off his body while Heston groaned and writhed with the pain and sank gasping to the ground. It later transpired that while laundering the clothes, somebody had dipped Heston's tights in kerosene. Since it was an outdoor production, both Macbeth and Banquo rode their horses bareback, and the sweat of the horses and the heat caused very nasty burns on Heston's legs and groin. Inquiries were made, but nobody knew who had done this or why or, more disturbingly, whether it had been an accident or an inexplicable piece of aggravation.

The curse was relentless that night, though it did exchange its physical malevolence for a more impish mood. The castle overlooked the sea and the ocean formed a very picturesque backdrop. It had been arranged that just before Lady Macbeth's death there

should be a loud scream and then a dummy wearing the same dress she had worn for the sleepwalking scene should be tossed off the rampart. It would sail down, catching the lights as it went out of sight into the sea below. Very dramatic, very convincing, very realistic. But in order to use the same dummy for each performance, it was attached by ropes to the rampart. On the opening night it was very windy. The scream came, the dummy was tossed fluttering through the air and down out of sight. Then, without missing a beat, the wind picked it up and it fluttered right back up again, landing with a loud plop at the feet of the actor who, as the messenger, was trying to say, "The queen is dead, my lord!". The audience naturally screamed with laughter.

Pain, and ridicule, and now confusion. The soldiers storming Macbeth's castle quite literally burned it down to the ground. Logs, faggots, and various complex wooden structures had been placed round the set and soaked in kerosene. When the soldiers stormed on, they lit everything with their flaming torches. Once again, this was an effect which would have been exceedingly impressive if all had gone according to plan, but in that high wind, the flames and smoke blew straight into the audience and caused a stampede as people screamed in panic and distress. Order was eventually restored, but the burning of the castle did not take place again.

The curse had one more trick up its sleeve. In spite of some impressive acting, the audience was finding it difficult to take the production seriously and were in that slightly hysterical mood when anything appears to be funny. Their final joy was at the end when Macduff brings Macbeth's severed head onto the stage on a long pole.

Heston had just played the part on television and thoughtfully had brought along with him the severed head which the TV property department had made. When it appeared it was seen that it was a realistic replica of Heston's face covered with blood and looking very gory, but for some extraordinary reason the audience decided that this was the funniest thing since Charlie

Chaplin and screamed with joy. As with the burning castle, the severed head was never seen again.

But at least there had been no fatalities. John Gielgud's wartime appearance in the play must surely hold the record in this respect. With rehearsals, provincial tour, and West End run it occupied ten months, and it was a very hectic and troublesome period for all concerned. Gielgud had played the part once before at his first season at the Old Vic in 1930 when he was twenty-six and just starting in Shakespeare. Everybody assumed that he was terribly miscast, but he astonished everybody, public, critics, and even fellow actors, by being very good. James Agate, the oldest, toughest, and hardest to please of all the critics, was so impressed by the murder scene that he actually visited Gielgud backstage in his dressing room to tell him how good he was and to prophesy that he would not be able to keep it up, a distinctly rash and unprofessional thing for a critic to do. It seemed that Gielgud proved him wrong, for he was deluged by splendid notices, and the three-week run passed without trouble or incident.

But re-creating a successful performance twelve years later is very difficult and full of pitfalls. He had some distinguished names to support him, Gwen Frangcon-Davies and Leon Quartermaine, but the difficulties of wartime casting had resulted in a rather makeshift company of frustrated old actors who couldn't get into the war, as Gielgud himself later described it. The music was by William Walton, the sets by John Minton, a brilliant young designer, and it was directed, rather unwisely, by Gielgud himself. Manchester in January 1942 was miserably cold, and the company had to battle through the ice, snow, and a blizzard to reach the gloomy and unheated Scala Theatre where the rehearsals were held. It was here that the first fatality occurred. Beatrice Fielden-Kaye, a splendid actress, who had been rehearsing the Third Witch, had been forced to leave the company. She had been feeling very ill, but she insisted on coming to the theatre every day to watch the rehearsals, wrapped up in furs and being made much of by the company. On the final Friday night she

died in her hotel from a heart attack. Tactfully, the company kept the news from Gielgud until after the opening five days later.

Older actors—there were many of them—shook their heads gloomily and talked about the curse and waited nervously for further trouble which was not long in coming. One by one the younger actors in the company dropped out, either for the army or from illness, and in Edinburgh the actor who played Duncan, Marcus Barron, died of angina pectoris. The play opened in July 1942 at the Piccadilly Theatre to rather mixed notices. Gielgud was dissatisfied with his own performance, Gwen Frangcon-Davies, a small-sized actress from South Africa, was dwarfed by the impressively somber settings, and the obvious miscasting was now clear to everybody.

William Walton's music was greatly admired by Gielgud and the audiences, but rather less so by the Three Witches who had to dance round the caldron rather more quickly than was comfortable to one of his more agitated musical frenzies, *presto agitato con fuoco*. Breathless, panting, and sweating, it was a nightly ordeal. Annie Esmond, one of the witches, could not keep up with the relentless tempo, and one night she collapsed on the stage and died.

John Minton later committed suicide in his studio surrounded by his pre-Raphaelite designs for the *Macbeth* sets and costumes. The flats used in the production were subsequently repainted for a light comedy which was sent out on tour. The star of the play was the charming and greatly loved Owen Nares, who was known as the first matinee idol. It was on this tour that he died.

The effectiveness of the curse is naturally dependent on the number of performances the play receives. It is no coincidence that the curse is most active in England and America where the play is seldom off the stage. On the Continent and in other foreign countries, *Macbeth* is not by any means the most popular Shakespeare play, so performances are rare and there are very few—and sometimes no—examples of trouble. In Russia, a performance of *Macbeth* is a rarity. There have been only two since

World War II, and Russian theatre people are politely surprised that the play is considered unlucky. It is also possible that the curse is less active where the play is in translation, since these will not be the words Shakespeare wrote. However, there have been some notable examples of bad luck on the Continent, so it would seem that translation carries no guarantee of immunity.

The earliest production of the play outside England was in Amsterdam in 1672 when a Dutch actor, Jan de Hoffmeyr, played the part with one of the actresses in his company whose husband was playing Duncan. Relations between the two men became worse, and shortly after the first performance, Jan de Hoffmeyr substituted a real dagger for the artificial one for the Duncan death scene which took place on the stage in full view of the audience. Duncan's death that night was horribly blood-stained and real. Jan de Hoffmeyr was arrested and served a life imprisonment.

Two generations of Greek actors have suffered at the hands of the play. Dimitri Murat, who had his own theatrical company in Athens, has recorded the disasters which he and his grandfather experienced.

After playing many heroic parts with his own theatre company, my grandfather decided to include *Macbeth* in his repertory, as he was very fond of this famous and excellent tragedy. Disaster! He was obliged to disband his company after years of lucrative touring and he realised that the bad luck was due to this ominous play. In the following year he formed a new company but as soon as he repeated *Macbeth* the bad luck returned. So, not willing to give up a play he loved so much, he assigned the part of Macbeth to a minor actor in his troupe, thinking thus he could avoid misfortune. He was wrong for the bad luck persisted. Finally he was forced to give up the play. My grandmother used to say that if it had not been for *Macbeth* they would have been rich.

It seems that I did not learn from the unlucky experiences of my grandfather. In 1956 I decided to produce *Macbeth* in the Rex Theatre in Athens which I had been managing for seven years. From that day on there was trouble between myself and the owner of the theatre, so that I was ultimately compelled to resign. It took me two years to recover from the reverse and I can assure you that I will never again try to perform this marvelous but unlucky play.

Stanislavski had always been fascinated by the play and spent many years preparing and rehearsing it with his Moscow Arts company. Russian indecisiveness and procrastination, in addition to the usual accompanying trouble, caused endless delays and postponements, but in the early 1900s, the production was declared ready and a grand dress rehearsal was held. In the murder scene, Macbeth suffered an alarming lapse of memory and, as was the custom in the turn-of-the-century Russian theatre, went down to the prompter's box for help. No prompt. He called out to the prompter. No reply. He stamped his foot angrily. Still nothing. Finally he investigated and found the old man slumped over the script—dead. With appropriate Russian fatalism, Stanislavski took the hint. He abandoned the production and never attempted it again.

A similar decision was made by the Portugese National Theatre in 1964 when Michael Benthall was invited to direct *Macbeth*, in translation, in Lisbon as Portugal's contribution to the Shakespeare centenary. It was a superb production, splendidly acted and received enthusiastic notices, but two days after the opening the theatre was burned down and it was six years before it was rebuilt. The production was abandoned, and suggestions that it be revived in the new house have been coldly received.

But there was nothing cold about the reception given to a Japanese production which may have been given in Japan some years ago. Legend has it that prisoners condemned to death were compelled to rehearse and play Macbeth with a company of professional actors, and that Macbeth's death by decapitation and the subsequent exhibition of his bleeding head on a pole was not faked. The production played as many performances as there were condemned prisoners. They were widely attended and received with enormous enthusiasm, since the spectacle of combining punishment with popular entertainment appealed strongly to the Oriental sense of justice. It is not, alas, known just how much truth there is in this exceedingly gruesome story, but anybody who suffered under Japanese hands in the wartime prison camps will have no trouble in believing it.

In view of the number of cancellations, it is amazing that *Macbeth* has ever reached the screen at all. In fact it has been filmed more than any other Shakespeare play, and the reference books list among them no less than nine, starting with an early silent version made in 1903 and starring Godfrey Tearle and Edmund Gwenn and finishing with Roman Polanski's recent version starring Jon Finch and Francesca Annis. The curse is just as active in the film studios as it is in the theatre. None has been really successful, and all have run into some sort of trouble.

Godfrey Tearle, fighting on top of a building, was nearly killed in his death throes, and Edmund Gwenn sustained injuries that caused pain to him for the rest of his life. Sir Herbert Beerbohm Tree, touring in America, made his Hollywood debut in a studio-shot version which was such a disaster that a ten-week season in New York was cut short after six days and his three-year contract was canceled. The film has, unhappily, vanished without a trace and that is a great loss, because on the evidence of what has survived of the film of his Svengali, Sir Herbert's highly melodramatic style did transfer rather effectively to the screen.

When Orson Welles finished his 1946 version, he discovered that the Scots accent which he had asked his actors to adopt was totally incomprehensible, and the sound track had to be entirely, and expensively, rerecorded. A Russian version was to have been filmed in Georgia, but nine members of the crew died of food poisoning while on location. A fire in the MGM studios in Hollywood in 1969, which destroyed millions of dollars worth of equipment, was finally traced to a cigarette lying on a wooden

*Sir Herbert Beerbohm Tree as Macbeth, with Constance Collier
as Lady Macbeth*

desk in the producer's office. The desk contained a large pile of shooting scripts for a projected version of *Macbeth*. The Polanski film is certainly the best to date, but this ran into serious trouble. Polanski was sacked by the distributors because he was way behind schedule, but after a long and critical interregnum he was reinstated.

Only when the film has nothing to do with Shakespeare does it escape the curse; to rehash the plot and transfer it to an another place and another time in history is perfectly safe. This explains the artistic success and untroubled shooting of two well-known very popular films, the Japanese version *Throne of Blood*, which has garnered well-deserved awards all over the world, and a modern, Chicago-based gangster version made in 1955 called *Joe Macbeth* starring Paul Douglas and Bonar Colleano. This escape route has been followed by the famous Zulu version *Umbatha*, in which the plot is transferred to a South African setting, intermittently follows Shakespeare with occasional patches of Zulu dialogue, but offers, as its chief attraction, a truly magnificent display of native dancing whose high spots are the play's dramatic climaxes. This, after huge success in South Africa, was the principal attraction of the 1971 World Theatre Season in England.

Another reason for the bad luck has been advanced by Michael Blakemore, and this is a strictly rational explanation dealing purely with the theatrical practicalities. *Macbeth* is virtually a one-part play. The imbalance is greater than in any other Shakespeare play, for the central character carries the lion's share of the dramatic burden, while the others are small parts standing round to feed him. Of these there are three good supporting parts—Lady Macbeth, Banquo, and Macduff—while the rest are little better than walk-ons. Because they are so uninteresting it is very difficult to get good actors to play them, which is one reason why it is rare to find productions that are well acted and well balanced throughout.

On first glance, Macbeth appears to be a heavy villain on

simple operatic lines, and the play can be taken to be a straightforward thriller à la Hitchcock, with a few spectacular effects which the director looks forward eagerly to devising. The obvious and calculated theatricality of those fights, witches, black magic, and ghosts enthrall the imagination, and a series of beautiful and frightening effects are worked out. Both actor and director are thus deluded into underrating the play and its problems. Both are unpleasantly surprised. The director invariably runs into urgent technical difficulties, and I've never heard of a production that didn't. He finds that this wonderful theatricality of the play is mysteriously slipping away between his fingers. The magnificent effects are not happening. *Macbeth* has evaded him, but why?

The actor finds that Macbeth is not a straightforward operatic villain. He is infinitely complex and full of disturbing inconsistencies. Just how does an actor reconcile and make theatrical sense of a man who is simultaneously a successful soldier, a brutal murderer, and a henpecked husband? The language in which all this is to be conveyed is full of the most subtle imagery, difficult to understand, and difficult to put over. An actor needs to work very hard, to do a great deal of theatrical homework and thoughtful preparation to make sense of it, and yet not to lose the impulse and excitement that makes it interesting to watch. Romantic impulsiveness, instinct, and a talent for inspired improvisation are no substitute.

What happens in the usual production of *Macbeth* is that the lead actor playing Macbeth gets progressively more worried and neurotic as he finds the part not as easy as he thought, while the rest of the company, standing around for hours with very little to do, gets increasingly bored and irritable. When action comes, it's rushing across the stage with bits of branches and leaves to represent Birnam Wood and then the dashing and staggering of the typical stage battle. Most actors find this rather embarrassing. Depression and paranoia set in; before long everybody is at each other's throats and that leads to trouble. The part is so physically and emotionally exhausting that the actor playing Macbeth wears himself out because the part is a series of superb high spots with no valleys and resting places in between. And when the end comes, the exhausted actor then has to fight four duels one after the other, up and down steps, rostrums, and different levels, usually in the near dark. It's not in the least surprising that few productions take place without some broken arms, legs, gouged eyes, cuts, bruises, and stabbings.

All these problems and many others came bubbling to the surface at the Royal Court in 1928. Nothing had caused more speculation, amusement, and alarm than Barry Jackson's announcement that his forthcoming production of *Macbeth* would be in modern dress. This was the first. Soon it was to trigger off a series of modern-dress Shakespeare productions; it became the fashion, then it became a craze, and then finally it came to be taken for granted and has now become a commonplace. But in 1928 it was an exciting novelty.

Sir Barry Jackson was one of the most astute theatrical brains of the century. He gave *Back to Methusalah* to the public, he started the Malvern Festival, and his repertory theatre in Birmingham was to supply many of the stars who enriched the theatre between the two world wars. But here he was to make one of his rare mistakes. There were casting troubles from the start, for the whole project was arousing pockets of fierce resistance in the theatrical establishment and nobody wanted to play in a dinner jacket. The likely actors were all mysteriously unavailable and only the unlikely ones were interested. In desperation he engaged Eric Maturin, a much admired actor whose low-keyed realistic style was admirable in Galsworthy and other modern plays but was totally unsuited to Shakespeare. Maturin had never been in a Shakespeare play and had never even seen one, and for some extraordinary reason this was regarded by Jackson and his colleagues as an advantage.

Not that they were looking consciously for a gimmick, not Jackson, nor H. K. Ayliff, and certainly not Paul Shelving, the designer. They believed honestly and sincerely that to liberate Shakespeare from all his gaudy trappings was to do him a great service. They believed—so the idea ran—that if the audience saw familiar, everyday clothes and settings on the stage, they would thus be able to concentrate on the play without any distractions. An interesting theory, but it turned out very differently in practice. Admittedly, the audiences were used to modern, everyday clothes, *but not in Shakespeare,* and therein lay the rub. The Jackson triumvirate might have taken warning from the advance publicity which concentrated on the clothes to the total exclusion of everything else. It is doubtful if in the whole history of the theatre there has been so much eager speculation on what the actors would be wearing rather on what they would be doing. Further warning might well have been taken from the fact that most of the papers sent along their fashion columnists, as well as their dramatic critics, to the first night.

The physical troubles started immediately. The sets had been constructed in advance and the actors had the unusual luxury of rehearsing in front of them rather than the usual empty stage. In the first week, they started to fall down and collapse onto the company who sustained some rather serious injuries. A month of rehearsal took place in an atmosphere of tension and gloom, everybody wondering, as is always the case, what was going to happen next. It was a fire in the dress circle which mysteriously broke out during the Sunday before the opening when the theatre was closed. There was considerable damage, many seats were burned beyond use, and a fireman was nearly suffocated to death. Miraculously, the fire was extinguished in time, and replacement seats were found before the opening.

It was as bad as the critics anticipated. Far from being an unobtrusive background, the costumes captured everybody's fascinated attention and succeeded in totally distracting the audience from the play. Shakespeare lost on points; he just didn't stand a chance. Macbeth in plus fours wielding golf clubs was a vastly intriguing novelty, and how could you take seriously a Lady Macbeth in a cloche hat and a waistless beaded skirt (Molyneaux), reclining on a chaise longue, smoking a Balkan Sobranie from a long green cigarette holder, reading Michael Arlen's *The Green Hat* and listening to *Carmen* on a windup gramophone? But the loudest laughter was reserved for the soldiers in khaki uniforms and tin helmets, carrying rifles and Bren guns as if they were on loan from *Journey's End* at the Savoy. With the three witches dressed and equipped as charladies, complete with buckets and mops; Fleance in an Eton collar; champagne and pêche Melbas in the banqueting scene; plus a plethora of white ties and tails—it was obvious to the first-night audience that Shakespeare had been willfully sacrificed to a stunt, and Barry Jackson was honest enough to admit the failure of the experiment in his first-night curtain speech.

The only person who came out of the sorry mess with any credit was Olivier, then just turned twenty-one. He played Malcolm in a dinner jacket for the banqueting scene, wore silk pajamas and Charvet dressing gown for the murder, and a very natty check lounge suit for the England interlude. Whereas the others tried to make Shakespeare sound like Galsworthy, he made the words sound like Shakespeare and thus caught the eye of Basil Dean who proceeded to give him a taste of overnight stardom in and as *Beau Geste* at Her Majesty's Theatre a few months later. That this spectacular and much-publicized production was a total disaster was nobody's fault.

Another disaster no less unpleasant and traumatic was also at the Royal Court Theatre in 1966 but of a rather different sort. William Gaskill, one of the Royal Court directors, had invited Sir Alec Guinness to play Macbeth, who had eagerly accepted. It was not his first contact with the part. Before World War II, he had learned the part in four days when asked to replace an actor at Sheffield Rep who had been suddenly taken ill. Under the circumstances he appears to have done well, but the opportunity of bringing thirty years' experience to the problems of the part was not to be turned down. There was, however, a condition attached: that a suitable Lady Macbeth be found. It has always been a very difficult part to cast, and it is highly unlikely that Shakespeare had any realization of just what sort of casting problem he was bequeathing to posterity. Do you get a hag or a sexpot? A woman who can drive her warrior-husband to regicide by sheer force of personality must be a battle-ax, but she must also be able to project some sort of sensuality to explain the domination. Sarah Siddons was a good example of the first, and Sarah Bernhardt (also Francesca Annis in the Polanski film) a good example of the second. Clearly a combination of the two was the ideal, but whom?

Their choice was to cause enormous controversy and bad feeling. Simone Signoret, the French film star, clearly combined sexuality with leadership. It had been Guinness' suggestion and Gaskill liked it. After a few initial misgivings, she accepted it eagerly. She had never acted in Shakespeare, even in France, and had never seen or even read *Macbeth*, which was quaintly regarded by her colleagues as an advantage. In addition, there was a slight language problem. Her English was fluent enough off stage and had seen her happily through her big film success *Room at the Top*, but to make her stage debut in Shakespeare in a foreign language and a foreign city with a costar whose presence would inevitably guarantee the widest publicity argued either great courage or great foolhardiness. "I must have been mad," she said laconically to the press. Rehearsals took place in a strangely light-hearted atmosphere. "We don't have to behave as if we are in a church even if it is a tragedy," she said sensibly. When Guinness and Gaskill were challenged to defend their choice of actress, Guinness pointed out the well-known theory that the part of Lady Macbeth was inspired by Mary, Queen of Scots, whose mother was French, and the play clearly reflected the murder of Darnley. It was a great challenge and Simone Signoret impressed everybody by her determination and hard work. She had a blackboard permanently installed in her hotel bedroom on which she wrote out the particularly difficult passages:

What thou would'st highly,
That would'st thou holily; would'st not play false,
And yet would'st wrongly win;

tricky alliteration and cross rhythms which, as Guinness pointed out sympathetically, would twist the tongues of many experienced English actresses.

Within three days of opening the box office, the four-week limited run was totally sold out. The four weeks of rehearsals dragged out in a blaze of publicity and the production opened on a very gloomy, foggy night—a very Macbeth night, as the press dryly pointed out—October 20, 1966. The performance went smoothly and there were no accidents or physical disasters. Simone Signoret was clearly exceedingly nervous, though nobody blamed her, and it was noticed that Guinness offered a very gentlemanly helping hand in moments of crisis. But Ronald Bryden, then writing for the *Observer*, remembers that although it was difficult to understand everything she said, the audience, which had been very restless and coughing interminably, shuddered to a respectful silence whenever she appeared, a tribute not only to her film-star fame but also to her stage personality and charisma.

The notices were appalling. Never had there been such unanimity, such an avalanche of abuse and vituperation. The closest examination of the Royal Court files revealed only two kind words. The *Daily Telegraph* described it as "sound but emphatically plain," while Harold Hobson in the Sunday *Times* admitted that he had liked Simone Signoret's smile and enlarged on the point with his usual verbose and repetitive detail. Madame Signoret was doubtless gratified to be that week's Hobson's Choice, but she shrugged her shoulders with truly Gallic *je m'en foutisme* and continued to face her nightly ordeal.

The critics denounced two experimental aspects of the production: the use of three West Indian actors to play not only the three witches but also the murderers (increased to three) was dismissed as a pointless gimmick and greeted with a tornado of jealous anger by the colored theatrical community. The set, which consisted of an open, unfurnished stage surrounded by three sandy-colored flats with bright unchanging lighting, was regarded as dull and unhelpful. Certainly it cannot be denied that the lack of any visual appeal or aids did throw an even greater strain than is usual on the acting abilities of the company.

Gaskill's reaction was an instant declaration of war. He wrote a scathing letter to the *Evening Standard* whose critic, Milton Shulman, had described the production as "a pretentious shambles." Gaskill protested against the cheap journalism that passed as criticism and announced his intention of banning the critics from all future Royal Court productions. In years to come similar threats were to be made by Royal Court directors, but in 1966 it had the air of novelty. The battle raged furiously for weeks, and relations between Fleet Street and Sloane Square reached its lowest-ever point. Gaskill was then invited to discuss the matter on television and was asked by Milton Shulman why he had selected a French actress who, whatever her talents and fame, couldn't speak English well enough to do justice to the part. "Because in my opinion, no English actress is capable of playing it," was his cool, calm reply.

This was indeed putting the cat in with the pigeons and the result was predictably frenzied. From the angry letters to the press and the Royal Court office, and the headlines following them, there was the inescapable conclusion that the English theatre was thickly populated with Lady Macbeths, both potential and actual. Gaskill diplomatically qualified his statement by announcing that the four-week season would be extended with Maurice Roeves and Susan Engels, who had been playing the Macduffs, promoted to the Macbeths. At the same time, Alfred Eisdale and Neville Blond, the chairman and deputy chairman of the Royal Court, announced that the ban on the critics was none of their seeking and that they would be invited as usual. There was some talk of William Gaskill resigning in protest, but he was persuaded to stay, and once again peace reigned in Sloane Square. However, a projected film version of the production, to be filmed as a straight photo of the play inside the theatre by Peter Snell who had recently filmed Frank Dunlop's no less controversial production of *The Winter's Tale*, was finally abandoned.

There are few actors who do not lust to play the part, whose great ambition is not to be able to shout out "Lay on, Macduff/ and damn'd be him that first cries 'Hold, enough!'" But it is a case of many being called and precious few being chosen. The artistic disasters can have a truly lethal effect on an actor's career. Lionel Barrymore satisfied a lifelong ambition in the early twenties and was torn to pieces by the critics with a viciousness that was unusual even for them. It killed his stage career, for he left Broadway and went to Hollywood, and never set foot on the stage again for the rest of his life. His brother John had always wanted to do the part, and there were many offers, but, with the calamitous experiences of Lionel fresh in his memory, he always refused. The sad case of Basil Langton is a typical example of how the curse can have an adverse effect on an actor's career. He had always wanted to play it, and in 1950 he had his chance at the Downtown Theatre, off-Broadway. The director was Ray Boyle and his Lady was Gerry Jedd. From the start, he remembers, everything went wrong. There was trouble over the cast, over the contracts, and over the production. As the opening drew nearer, his wife advised him to get out of the production while he could. He refused. The opening night was a disaster, and at the party afterward some amiable fool put on the finishing touches by saying, "You really did something for me, Basil. For the first time in my life I felt really sorry for Macbeth." The critics treated him very badly, the notices were really crucifying, and the worst was from Walter Kerr who had previously been a great friend. This finished the friendship and it also finished his acting career. He did do a little afterward, but the desire and impulse had gone. He then moved over to direction which he now does very successfully.

Broadway has never been very hospitable to *Macbeth* which has seldom enjoyed success there. The traditional situation in England, that whatever physical and artistic disasters are in attendance, the public always flocks to see it, doesn't seem to apply in New York, where short runs are the rule. Gladys Cooper and her husband Phillip Merivale, in all their dual glory, couldn't make it run for more than a week in 1934. Walter Hampden's revival of the same year survived only four performances and is remembered by Walter Kerr chiefly for the interminable gaps when the curtain was lowered after every scene to allow complicated changes. Hampden had been unusually unlucky with the play which had always been a favorite. He presented it three times on Broadway; the first in 1918 survived only a single performance and the second in 1921 only six.

In 1970, Rip Torn rehearsed what promised to be a very interesting experimental production which eliminated a number of small parts, cut the play down to a straight two hours, and kept Macbeth on the stage throughout. Just before the opening, the off-Broadway actors went on strike for more money and better conditions, the theatres were all closed and *Macbeth* was canceled. In the following year there was a production at the Mercer O'Casey Theatre starring David Leary which surely breaks some sort of record for damage. Within three months there had been a fire that destroyed scenery, furniture, and properties. There were no less than seven robberies in the course of which the hooligans tore out all the telephones from the walls, slashed the gauze scrims, made a bonfire of all the costumes and caused a financial loss of $80,000.

And let it not be forgotten that it was during a performance of *Macbeth* that the historic Astor Place riot in 1849 took place. Edwin Forrest, the leading American tragedian, was supposed to have organized it against William Macready, his hated English rival, then on an extended American tour. Hundreds of patriotic Forrest supporters pelted the English actor with tomatoes and manure, thus forcing him off the stage. Outside, the military was ordered to fire above the rioting crowd reported to be 20,000 strong, but owing to the confusion of the moment, the soldiers fired into the crowd. Thirty-one people were killed. It must also be remembered that *Macbeth* was Abraham Lincoln's favorite play, and that the day before the assassination he was reading aloud one of his favorite passages to a party of friends while sailing down the Potamac on the riverboat *Queen:*

> Duncan is in his grave;
> After life's fitful fever he sleeps well;
> Treason has done his worst: nor steel, nor poison,
> Malice domestic, foreign levy, nothing
> Can touch him further!

The story of the Macbeth curse is a grim one, but even the murkiest subject can have its lighter side, and it is fitting that this investigation should be concluded on a note of comedy. Actors are fond of telling stories of the legendary Sir Peregrine Plinge who once played the part. He was not ideal casting at the best of times, and these times were not of the best, for he was tired and not in good health. He was deeply unhappy about his performance and throughout the season would indulge in long orgies of self-lacerating masochism. One night, when waiting in the wings, he approached his Macduff. "Give me five pounds," he said. Macduff was very startled by this. "I beg your pardon, Sir Peregrine; *what* did you say?" "Give me five pounds," repeated the knight. "But why?" asked the bewildered Macduff. "Because if you don't," said Sir Peregrine, "I shall tell everybody that you played Macduff to my Macbeth." On another occasion he was seen soliloquizing in the canteen. "I'm a terrible Macbeth, the worst Macbeth that ever was. If I was a member of the public, I'd go and ask for my money back." He then went to the box office and added another item to the local mythology. "I want my money back," he said to the startled girl. "This is without exception the very *worst Macbeth* I have ever seen." The girl was new to the theatre and didn't recognize him, but she knew her business and politely refused. Whereupon, in his best Alice-in-Wonderland manner, he wandered off still muttering, "the worst *Macbeth* in history; it's a disgrace!"

During the thirties, when Dame Edith Evans was enriching the theatre with a superb Katharine and a marvelous Rosalind, she was asked if she would like to play Lady Macbeth. "It's absolutely out of the question," she replied in that unique voice, "I could *never* impersonate a woman who had such a *peculiar* notion of hospitality." It was a Thursday evening at Chichester that an American couple were watching *Macbeth* from the front row of the stalls. The famous soliloquy "tomorrow and tomorrow and tomorrow" started, whereupon the American wife turned to her husband. "Do you get it, Hank?" she whispered loudly. "That means Sunday!"

But certainly the funniest of the *Macbeth* stories, and one which makes a fitting conclusion to this investigation deals with an ambitious but not overtalented young actor who was employed in Sir Donald Wolfit's traveling Shakespeare Company. His contribution to *Macbeth* was as the final messenger who has to run on stage and stammer out, "My Lord, the queen is dead," and then run away. For many seasons he did just this, and then he became bored and asked Sir Donald if he could play a larger part. Wolfit refused. The young actor continued to ask and Wolfit continued to refuse. The young actor became increasingly depressed and the matter developed into an obsession. Thoughts of revenge filled his waking hours and one evening he decided to sabotage the play. That night he ran onto the stage. "My Lord," he shouted, "the queen is *much better and is even now at dinner.*" He then ran off, leaving the astonished actor-manager to deal with the situation as best he could.

To all who have helped I say thank you very much:

Franklin Cover, New York; Walter Kerr, New York; Clive Barnes, New York; Trader Faulkner, London; John Nettleton, London; Brigid Skemp, London; Jay Fox and Bonnie Walker Fox, New York; Reńe Rosen, New York; Don Bonnell, New York; John Graham, London; Magdalen Egerton, London; Nicholas Hawtrey, London; Hugh Goldie, London; Jim Dale, London; John Bennett, London; Jill Bennett, London; Dr. Levi Fox, Stratford on Avon; Ian Richardson, London; Michael Denison, London; Dulcie Gray, London; Thora Hird, London; Joe Melia, London; Hersey Pigot, London; Anthony Tuckey, Liverpool; Peter Hall, London; Joseph Fox, London; Ken Wynne, London; Professor A. N. Kincaid, Oxford; Robert Gillespie, London; Peter Porteous, London; Michael Gambon, London; Geoffrey Bayldon, London; Donald Laye-Smith, London; Mrs. Barbara Richards, South Africa; Christine Hole, Oxford.

Hugh Cross, London; Paul Hardwick, London; Michael Warwick, London; Frank Seton, London; James D. P. Smith, Bushey; William Abney, London; Max Miradin, London; Angela B. Hill, Shadwell; Barry Foster, London; Stan Turney, London; Martin Jarvis, London; Fitzroy Davis, New York; Melinda May, London; John Maas, Philadelphia; Jane and Francis Carr, London; Nigel Hawthorne, London; George Baker, London; Roger Lancelyn-Green, Wirral; Michael Goodliffe, London; Fred Lawrence Guiles, New York; Bridget Boland, London; Marianne and Barrie Hesketh, Isle of Mull; E. Hardman, Widnes; Abraham Sofaer, New York; J. M. G. Blakiston, Oxford; George Hagan, London; John Haylock, Brighton; Tony Britton, London; Harry Tuthill, Cape Town; Eva Bornemann, Germany; Herb Moulton, Vienna; Franz Schrafranek, Vienna.

Robert Rushmore, Massachusetts; Michael Harnick, Bronx; Jutta Grunthal, Haifa; Olive Peel, Durban; Ruby Betts, Utica; Oleg Kerensky, London; Sir Alec Guinness, London; Spike Hughes, Ringmer; David Shipman, London; Jean McConnell, Tonbridge; Vera Lindsey, London; Richard Schenkman, Yonkers; Anne Harlan, New Haven; Kathie Warren, High Barnet; A. J. Beale, Walton-on-Thames; Hugh Beeson, Jr., New York; Brendan Gill, New York; Vi Marriott, London; Jack Lyne, London; Walter Horsburgh, London; Bernard Archard, London; Jack Lemmon, California; Henry Marshall, London; Richard Attenborough, Richmond Green; Sheila Campbell, New York; Ellen Pollock, London; Patricia Hayes, London; Clive Revill, London; Laurence Irving, Tenterden; Dudley Moore, London; Paul Myers, New York; Bob Thomas, California; Zena Dare, London; John Mills, London; Sir Robert Helpmann, London.

Robert Potterton, Dublin; Denis Shaw, Windsor; Wilfrid Granville, London; Renée Bourne Webb, London; Tenniel Evans, Bucks; David Williams, Liverpool; Michael Codron, London; John Savident, London; T. Robertson, Stalybridge; Emlyn Williams, London; Donald Sinden, London; Ronald Harwood, West Liss; Robert Selbie, Chichester; Jean Kent, London; Enid St. John Parry, Somerton; Patlick MacClellan, Isle of Man; Derek Fowldes, London; Sir Laurence Olivier, Brighton; Peter Saunders, London; Eric Paice, West Wratting; Leslie Phillips, London; Paul Huson, New York; Amanda Reiss, London; Peter Barkworth, London.

John Shrapnel, London; Clayre Ribner, New York; Gerald Blake, New York; Julia Jones, London; Charles Lewson, London; Barry Morse, London; Anthony Quayle, London; Elizabeth Armstrong, Harrogate; Armand Georges, Rickmansworth; Michael Hordern, London; Dennis Wheatley, London; Graham Beynon, Loughborough; Frank Thornton, London; J. K. Hunt, Warwick; Maureen Norman, Great Yarmouth; Peter Bull, London; Charles Bowden, London; Kenneth Tynan, London; Otto G. Stoll, New Jersey; Ted Gilling, London; Jack Doughty, Oldham; A. L. Rowse, Oxford; Sandy Dunbar, London; Geoffrey Toone, London; John Drummond, Isle of Man; B. M. Hancock, Birmingham; Margaret Rawlings, Wendover; Viscount Furness, London; S. W. Milverton, Oldham; Edgar Wreford, London; Sharon Duce, London; T. R. Goulding, Blackpool; Margaret Webster, U.S.A.; Tony Robinson, Port Elizabeth; Sir John Gielgud, London; Andrew Cruikshank, London; David Rustidge, Oldham; Stephen Tate, York; Robert Perfitt, St. Neots; Miss H. Crompton, Oldham; J. Clegg, Liverpool.

Robert Morley, Wargrave; C. Birchenough, Maulsfield; Patrick Garland, London; Meryl Wold, Denver; Eric Porter, Stratford on Avon;

Nicholas Grimshaw, Richmond; Judy McKeown, London; A. V. Dalby, London; Brigit Ferguson, Lamberhurst; William Redfield, New York; Jack Fletcher, New York; Frederick Teahan, New York; Dimitri Murat, Athens; A. R. James, Ovingdean; Arnold Gates, New York; Theodore Hoffman, Brooklyn; Kay Ward, Columbus; Phillip Weller, Washington, D.C.; George Nestor, Lambs Club, New York; William Shust, Players Club, New York; Sandy Marshall, Lambs Club, New York; Frank Alford, Lambs Club, New York; Bill Buckley, Lambs Club, New York.

Alan Hewitt, New York; Emerson Beauchamp, Washington, D.C.; Louis Marder, Chicago; Catherine Hughes, New York; David Leonard, Ballet Bookshop, London; John O'Brien, Ballet Bookshop, London; Michael Sinclair, New York; Bob Pearce, Kuala Lumpur; Margaretta Scott, London; John Harrison, High Wycombe; Arne Meier, London; P. Murray-Hoodless, London; P. W. Janes, Farningham; Paul Rogers, London; Ian Holm, London; Raymond Adamson, Beckenham; John Woodvine, London; Derek Salberg, Salisbury; J. G. Trewin, London; John Moffatt, London; Fred Marshall, Colchester; Gill Rutter, Egham; John Irwin, London; Timothy Schultz, Williamstown; Leda Sulta, New York; H. Clarke, Eastbourne; Lyell Rodieck, New York; Mrs. Elsie Hawksworth, London; J. Almieda Flor, Lisbon; R. A. Cable, Dover; Robin Hood, London; Mary Lynn, London; Margaret Ware, Huddersfield; Brenda Cleather, London; Meg Ritchie, London; George Manuel, Cape Town; Clara Hackett, New York; Victor Lownes, London; Douglas Emory, Beckenham; Mrs. D. Beckett, Eastbourne; Noel Johnson, London; Cardew Robinson, London; Richard Dennis, London.

Ann Rogers, London; John Bryans, London; Michael Ridgeway, London; Gerry Small, London; John Moore, London; June Grey, London; Herb Felsenfield, Milwaukee; Bob Hoskins, London; Stephen Mead, London; William Lewis, New York; Dennis Handby, London; Basil Langton, New York; Marjorie Beddow, New York; Jeanne Belkin, Brooklyn; Bill Lemessina, New York; Barbara Rubinstein, New York; David Cattanach, New York; Joe Wiebkin, Fulham.